DEFYING DEATH

Zakaria Botross - Apostle to Islam

A biography by Stuart Robinson
with Peter Botross

DEFYING DEATH

Zakaria Botross - Apostle to Islam

A biography by Stuart Robinson
with Peter Botross

CityHarvest
Publications

This book is dedicated to all those followers of Jesus who have been deployed on difficult assignments, who for the time being must remain nameless, but who are already well known as heroes in heaven.

ENDORSEMENTS - The Life of an Extraordinary Christian

Father Zacharia Botross is a skilled exegete pounding home applications in the dramatic oratorical manner of the great pulpit ministers ... At times he is a fiery evangelist ... At times he also becomes a holiness preacher ... He is one of the most powerful ministers of the Word of God we have ever heard.

Edward Plowman
Christianity Today
News Editor (April 1978)

"Silenced by the Church for years for rediscovering and preaching ancient truths, jailed for ministering to Muslims, "exiled" from Egypt to Australia, establishing a phenomenal church in England, freed to unleash his life long vision at 70, words can hardly describe the amazing life of Zakaria Botross.

Today millions of Muslims watch his satellite programmes and visit his website. Countless thousands across the Arabic speaking Islamic world are turning to Christ because of his ministry. His life is littered with miracles and mayhem, daring danger and defying death. Reading this book will take you where you've never been before."

Dr. Pat Robertson
Founder Christian Broadcasting Network (CBN)

"Nearly fourteen centuries ago Arab armies swept out from Arabia and within one hundred years overran formerly Christian countries from Afghanistan in the east to Morocco in the west. They impressed on local populations a new religion - Islam. With time the church mostly ceased to exist in those countries.

But today God is reversing that trend. Muslims are turning to Christ. This is dangerous for the new believer and the messenger of Jesus, but Zakaria Botross doesn't avoid danger. Through his unique ministry thousands of Muslims in the Arab world are coming to Christ. Read his story and be inspired by the God of the impossible."

Dr. George Hill
California Victory Church
Founder of Victory Churches International

"Stuart Robinson has done a valuable service to the Christian church in bringing the life of this extraordinary Christian to our attention. Read it, and imagine what might happen to your church, your city, even your nation should God find the availability of a Zakaria Botross in us."

Dr. Allan Meyer
Careforce Church
Melbourne Australia

Father Zakaria's ministry through Life (Al-Hayat) Television Channel has deeply impacted millions of people throughout the Middle East and Europe. This pioneering ministry has challenged Islam in the Arab world like never before. The tide has turned after 14 centuries of ignorance. Fr. Zakaria and his challenging questions of Islam are the central topics of conversations in homes, cafes, taxis, political circles and in the Islamic national and international Media. Entire programs on Islamic Television are dedicated to discussing the questions raised by Fr. Zakaria Botross.

Television hosts have publicly criticized Islamic scholars for their inability to offer adequate answers to the questions presented through Life (Al-Hayat) Channel. Father Zakaria's courageous ministry has changed the way many Muslims and Christians view Islam, prompted Muslims to investigate hard questions and opened the doors wide for thousands of people to come to a saving knowledge of Jesus Christ. Fr. Zakaria's ministry has challenged and changed many Christians to live an active witness in their unreached communities. History will record the incredible impact and revolution in mission especially the eternal outcome of Fr. Zakaria's ministry to Muslims worldwide.

Defying Death is an outstanding and faith inspiring book. It gives the reader a glimpse of what the God of the supernatural is doing in the Arab Muslim world and how one man's life has changed the destiny of thousands across many continents.

Abo Ali
Producer of Al-Hayat Life TV- Satellite
Channel (Arabic programs) Europe.

Published by CityHarvest Publications

PO Box 6462
Upper Mt Gravatt Australia

www.cityharvest.org.au
chp@cityharvest.org.au

ISBN 0-9775602-2-8

Unless otherwise noted, scripture quotations are from the Holy Bible, New International Version. Copyright 1973, 1978, 1984, International Bible Society.

Printed in Australia.

Cover Design & Layout by David Gray for www.mooloolabaweb.com

CONTENTS

EDITOR'S NOTE

The tattoo of the cross:

When Islam spread in Egypt in the 7th Century, Christians adopted this 'sign' for the purpose of identification with Jesus. It is a public declaration that a person is 'proud' of following Jesus and accepts to carry the cross! Today Christians in Egypt still use the tattoo to declare that:

- they are Christians,
- they are proud of their cross (representing their saviour and persecution) and
- they are not 'fearful' of being identified publicly regardless of threats, humiliation, loss of privileges, even death.

INTRODUCTION

When British Christian scholar, evangelist, pastor and teacher John Stott visited a mid-week meeting in Cairo in the 1970s, he was deeply impressed. Decades later in 2002 he still recalled the event. In his book, *People My Teachers* Stott wrote:

> One of the most striking figures of the Coptic Orthodox Church at that time was Abuna (Father) Zakaria Botross. He was an Orthodox priest who in 1964 had an evangelical experience of Christ, which changed the direction of his ministry. He was now expounding Scripture and answering questions to one thousand or more people using relay and closed circuit television, every Tuesday and Thursday evening in the hall of his church, St. Marks. Some friends and I attended a part of his meeting one Thursday evening. He was faithfully expounding Galatians 5 and 6 (pp 41-42).

Stott was not the only one to be impressed. The *World Christian Encyclopaedia (Oxford University Press N.Y. p.278)* recorded:

> In 1978 a new renewal movement, including tongues, healings and other charismatic phenomena, emerged at St. Mark's Church, Heliopolis, under the leadership of a priest, Father Zakaria Botross, attracting weekly crowds of 3,000 and baptising 200 converts from Islam.

In that same year, Edward Plowman, news editor for *Christianity Today,* in that magazine's April edition (p.58), wrote:

> Father Zakaria Botross, 44, steps to the podium and opens his Bible ... Taller than average, he immediately commands attention. A hundred tape recorders are immediately clicked on ... Father Zakaria ... amplifies each point with illustrations ... pounding home applications in the dramatic oratorical manner of the great pulpit masters. At times he is a fiery evangelist ... At times he is a skilled exegete ... At some points he also becomes a holiness preacher ... All

over the auditorium people pray ... Some openly weep ...
He is one of the most powerful ministers of the Word we
have ever heard.

Not only did Fr Zakaria preach for conversions to Christ and to
strengthen believers, he also effectively rebutted accusations against
Christianity made by Islamic leaders. He presented arguments, which
challenged them to re-examine the question of the validity of their
religion, their Holy book the Quran, and their prophet Mohammad.

The conversion of Muslims to Christianity or to any other religion puts
at risk the lives of the converts and the ones responsible for such
"apostasy". Even questioning the teachings of Islam and its practices
can have dire consequences.

Fr Zakaria's zealous activities could not help but attract the notice of
authorities of the State, of the Islamic leadership and of those within
his own church. He was stood down from his position within the Coptic
Church. In 1980 and 1989 he endured imprisonment. Then he was
deported into exile from Egypt. His subsequent ministry in Australia
and England was attended with great success but not with everyone's
approval.

Today in his eighth decade, he lives with a degree of security in the
United States of America. He exercises a worldwide ministry especially
through satellite broadcasting made possible through the generosity of
friends in his latest "homeland".

But various reports from reliable sources indicate that a multimillion
dollar price (a fatwa), has been placed upon his head as a bounty
for any who may kill him. This is because his ministry to Muslims is
so challenging, effective and productive. If his arguments can't be
countered then his voice must be silenced. Throughout his trials, his
family has been threatened and has suffered also. Only very recently,
the last of his immediate family has been removed from Egypt to a
safer location. Numerous TV shows in Cairo have attacked him. Four
books in Arabic have been written against him by Islamic leaders.

Many years before she would meet and marry Fr Zakaria, his wife to
be, Violet, had a vivid dream that deeply moved her. In her dream she
saw herself in a deserted place. Suddenly heaven above opened and
released a small cross and a picture of Mary the mother of Jesus,

recognised by Coptic Christians as a holy icon. As she ran to pick up the cross, a loud voice thundered, "No, don't pick it up. It's too heavy to carry. Take the icon instead." After fifty years of ministry with her husband which has been characterised by much affliction, imprisonments, humiliations, separation from children and relatives, excruciating loneliness and attendant stress, she and they well understand what it means to live in the shadow of the cross.

You are about to discover how God uses an ordinary person to achieve extraordinary outcomes, probably never achieved before in 1400 years of ministry to Muslims. If God can do this with one 'untrained' individual perhaps he wants to do the same with you too!

When Fr Zakaria's youngest son Peter, was only four years old, he sat captivated on his mother's lap in church listening intently to his father's retelling the dramatic post-resurrection encounter between Jesus and the Apostle Peter. In the retelling, Fr Zakaria called out the immortal words of Jesus, *"Peter, do you love me?"* (John 21:15-17). Immediately in the silence a squeaky four-year-old voice called back, "Yes, Dad, I do love you." Young Peter's spontaneity caused the crowd of thousands to erupt into uncontrollable laughter. Today countless thousands of others would hasten to add that they also love him.

As you read this book, you will come to know Fr Zakaria Botross and the Lord whom he serves – Jesus. May you also come to love them. This is their story.

PROLOGUE

The restaurant wasn't always this busy.

Tonight seemed to be one of those times when nearly everyone wanted to eat out and be served immediately. Not that the gentlemen at the quieter table off to one side had to worry. They were well known as good customers. Their waiter hovered attentively. He also unobtrusively listened to their conversation.

Their talk was about a fellow who was stirring up a lot of controversy. He was publicly challenging long-held unexamined claims and beliefs of Islam via satellite TV. It would be an honour to contribute toward getting rid of him. One of the men at the table offered 5 million Egyptian pounds to have the job done.

In a distant location, the room was quiet when the phone shrilled its interruption. The FBI was on the line. They had received notice from a reliable source that a man of Middle Eastern origin was making discreet inquiries. He was offering US$1 million just to find out the address of his target.

The FBI was assured that God was the best protector one could have. He had done quite a good job thus far. But to demonstrate their advice was appreciated and would be taken seriously, it was agreed that extra TV surveillance cameras and necessary security up-grades would be installed as soon as possible.

Life wasn't always as insecure as this. But after a lifetime of experience of attempting to reach Muslims for Jesus Christ, this sort of danger was hardly new to Zakaria Botross.

CHAPTER 1

OUT FROM OBSCURITY

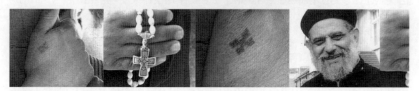

Beginnings

In the small village of Kafer El Dawar 40 kilometres from the Mediterranean city of Alexandria in northern Egypt, Anisa Girgius prayed and fasted. It had been 5 years since the birth of her second child and she longed for a third. In the large family home in which she lived with her husband, Henien Botross, there were five bedrooms. It was so big compared with other houses in the village, that it was later leased to become a village school. Surely God would want to bless her with more children to fill these rooms with pattering feet and happy laughter? To assist in drawing the attention of the Almighty to her situation, she even enlisted prayer support from her local church community.

On October 24 1934 her prayer was answered. Feyez Botross Henien Saad Dawoud was born. Ever generous to respond to the petitions of his people, God later added three more children to the family--Farooz, Maurice and Francis to join the older two, Mary and Phillip. The family home was in a relatively affluent area of the village. Henien had a steady income. He worked hard and did well. As a tax collector he was highly regarded because of his exceptional honesty.

Like all Middle Eastern fathers, Henien loved his son. He would do almost anything to please him. So when the four-year-old Feyez begged repeatedly for a pony, even this request was eventually granted.

Fathers good or bad, inevitably have a significant impact upon their children. Fortunately Henien's was good. He used to take his young son on business trips to Upper Egypt. Feyez was impressed with his father's love of hymn singing and his frequent recitation of Psalm 51. He observed his father always making the sign of the cross on his face with soap before washing it each morning. His father's simple declarations of submission to and trust in God deeply impressed young Feyez.

Henien had two other interests which impacted his son. The first was his love for Muslims and his desire to see them liberated from the bondage of Islam, to the freedom found in the Jesus whom he served. Feyez often listened in as Kamel Mansour, a former Muslim religious leader, was invited home to retell the story of his conversion to Christ.

The second area of interest was in the signs of the end of the world about which Jesus instructed his followers (Matthew 24). Some of the most notable battles of the Second World War were fought out on Egyptian soil. British General Montgomery's massed tanks fought desperately against the German army led by the "Desert Fox", the brilliant German commander General Rommel.

Not unnaturally many Christians in Egypt thought such unprecedented events indicated that the end of the world could be at hand. When Israel was re-established in 1948, certainty increased. Love for the conversion of Muslims and anticipation of the return of Jesus would later become two of the hallmarks of Feyez's ministry.

Henien's work responsibilities necessitated the growing family moving from Kafer El Dawar to Dalangat, Kom El Basel to Damanhoor. His experience of being frequently obliged to move was good training for the rigorous necessities of Feyez's later life and ministry.

In Kom El Basel not only did the family have a large home, they also had enough land to keep their own sheep for meat, cows for milk, chickens for eggs and a horse and donkeys for transport. Their own fruit trees and vegetable gardens also provided for the family's food needs. Just across the muddy road outside the home, was a small lake which became a swimming hole and fishing spot for the children. As there was no electricity, there were seldom arguments about what time was appropriate for each to go to bed.

Eight kilometres away was the Abo Hamera Church which had been built by the family's forebears. Distance meant attendance became irregular. The exceptions were special Sundays such as those of the pre-Easter Lenten season. After services, families always gathered outside the church to share fellowship meals together.

There being no formal educational facilities in Kom El Basel, young Feyez and his older brother Phillip were dispatched to the more distant town of Damanhoor. Their older sister Mary or their mother went with them and stayed to care for them in a rented apartment. Throughout the academic year the boys were permitted the joy of returning home only during the long summer vacation.

Even though by present standards Damanhoor was small with a population of only a few thousand, life seemed so different for a village boy. The town bustled with life. There seemed to be people everywhere. Feyez missed the freedom, solitude and relaxing simpler rural lifestyle. He also desperately missed his father and yearned to return home.

In Damanhoor Feyez had been enrolled in a Coptic school which had been established by El Jameya El Khayreia El Kepteya. This was the only school which taught Christian religious studies. Feyez also began attending Coptic Sunday school classes, although neither God nor church held too much personal interest for him as yet. But he was attracted to the disciplines and rewards of systematic study. The foundation was being laid for a lifelong practice.

It was at primary school Feyez met and befriended Joseph Habib. With mutual encouragement their friendly rivalry ensured that the two top academic places were awarded to them each year.

When Feyez was seven years of age his Syrian born teacher of English, Mr Gregory, explained the use of the words, "who, whom, which and that." Then he wrote incomplete sentences on the blackboard and asked the students to fill in the gaps. Most were unable to complete the task. But Feyez completed the assignment perfectly.

Duly impressed Mr Gregory enquired, "What does your father do for a living?"

"He's a tax collector," Feyez replied.

"Can he afford further education for you?"

"Yes, Sir," confidently answered young Feyez.

Mr Gregory, patting the boy on the shoulder said, "When you grow up, enrol yourself in a Bachelor of Arts degree majoring in English."

The boy never forgot his teacher's early advice and encouragement. Ten years later he did precisely as he had been instructed.

By the time Feyez was ready to advance to secondary school, stability and security once more had returned to his life. The entire family had moved to Damanhoor. But security of life and property is always fragile for the often oppressed minority Christian community in Muslim dominated Egypt.

Feyez had been greatly influenced by an older half-brother, Foad, who was a man of God not just in name. In the Coptic Church, men often entered the priestly office through the entitlement of inheritance rather than as a result of divine calling reinforced by spiritual and other complementary qualifications.

Many priests attended church to conduct mass, after which they would spend their days visiting people, collecting monies, indulging in drunken behaviour or whatever took their fancy. Somehow, in the midst of this, Foad had a life changing encounter with Jesus. From then on he enjoyed singing hymns, praying and reading the Bible. He travelled extensively, passionately preaching and teaching the Word of God. This brought him to the attention of more than Christian congregations.

One night as he returned from yet another preaching engagement, a group of Muslims ambushed him. They cut out his tongue to put an end to his preaching. Then they murdered him. Feyez was later presented with Foad's Bible. The blood of this martyr would water a seed planted deep within Feyez and would significantly determine the later course of his ministry.

Life Lessons

Life in Damanhoor was filled with lessons to be learned by the inquisitive, impressionable adolescent Feyez. One was that every opportunity, no matter how seemingly insignificant, could lead to greater benefits later on.

Beneath the apartment in which the Botross family lived, was a small shop which sold fava beans and falafel. Its owner, El Assee, had arrived in Damanhoor and applied for the job of cleaner in one of the local secondary schools. This was not a highly sought after position. Cleaners were frequently humiliated, poorly treated and paid very low wages. El Assee couldn't even obtain this much maligned job because he was illiterate. But he did know how to cook fava beans and falafel. He sold his product in sandwiches from a cart on a street corner.

Business boomed. Eventually he purchased a shop in a prominent location. His reputation grew. Finally he obtained a monopoly for supplying the royal household. Daily the king's car would make the 2 hour journey from Cairo to collect the consignment of El Assee's cooked beans. On one occasion when he visited his local bank to deposit a significant sum of money, the teller asked him to sign a deposit slip. El Assee stared at the teller and said, "If I was able to sign my name I wouldn't be here with this much money. I'd still be a school janitor!"

Feyez noted the results of El Assee's persistent labours. He learned from this that every opportunity no matter how small was to be eagerly grasped.

Joseph Habib and Feyez had gone to study at different secondary schools. In March 1950 they coincidentally met again at a local bean and falafel shop. Joseph proposed that they reunite for study purposes. Feyez readily agreed. Study alternated between their respective homes on a daily basis. Joseph's older brother Matta, tutored them in mathematics.

However Joseph refused to study on Thursdays and Fridays. On Thursday evenings he attended youth and Sunday school teachers' meetings. On Fridays he attended mass in the mornings and taught Sunday school in the afternoons. Feyez tried to persuade Joseph to restrict his church activities to summer vacations. Joseph countered with an invitation for Feyez to join him in attending church. Feyez refused. Academic study was his top priority and he would not deviate from it. On Thursdays and Fridays Feyez studied even more intensely so that on Saturdays he could pepper Joseph with difficult academic questions.

On June 1, 1950 both boys received their end of year results. They were both thrilled with the success they obtained. Journeying home, as they passed Joseph's church, he suggested they go in and together thank God for their excellent results. Feyez declined on the basis that he hadn't asked for God's help therefore there was no need to thank him. He suggested however that Joseph should, because even though he'd wasted two days a week, still he had passed well.

As Joseph left the church, Fr Boulos, the parish priest met him at the door. Joseph, pointing to his friend Feyez who was waiting for him on the other side of the road, told the priest how well Feyez also had passed the exams. Immediately Fr Boulos crossed the street, embraced Feyez and congratulated him.

Feyez was astonished at the spontaneous sincerity and fatherly love shown by the priest to a total stranger. When Fr Boulos invited Feyez to attend the youth and Sunday school teachers' meetings the next day, Feyez surprised himself by accepting. This would represent the commencement of a new stage in Feyez's development.

Ministry Begins

On Friday June 3, 1950 on the second day of his new association with church, Feyez agreed to teach a Year 8 Sunday school class. The night before he'd been given the relevant lesson printed on small sheets of green paper. The topic to be taught was, "The Sacraments of the Church". With his characteristic discipline for study, he memorised the material and enthusiastically went to teach his first class.

The Coptic Orthodox Church believes in seven sacraments: baptism (of infants), confirmation, repentance, eucharist, unction (anointing) of the sick, priesthood and matrimony.

When Feyez spoke of the sacrament of "matrimony" the children broke out into spontaneous laughter. There had been a spelling mistake in the lesson material. Instead of teaching about the sacrament of marriage, Feyez was inadvertently speaking about the sacrament of "heart attack". At least both concepts were matters relating to the heart.

One of the children finally let their new teacher in on the joke by telling him that the sacrament was marriage not "heart attack". Feyez was not open to correction. It wasn't so much that a spelling mistake in the text had led him into error. He just couldn't believe that marriage itself would actually be a sacrament of the church. To rescue his honour as a teacher, he showed the boy what it said in the printed lesson material and rebuked the boy for his rudeness in even suggesting that marriage could be a sacrament. His attempt to prove the correctness of his teaching only resulted in more gales of laughter from his greatly amused students. Feyez, due to his ignorance, obviously knew little of the church's teaching and only made matters worse by his insistence on teaching the material as printed.

Continued riotous laughter brought Fr Boulos speedily to the scene to gently correct the error of his newly recruited teacher. Deeply humiliated, Feyez learned an important lesson, never again to depend upon a single source of information when preparing to speak on any topic.

What would grow into half a century of ministry began on that day in St George's Church in Damanhoor. Feyez began regular Bible study, fasting and church attendance, as he strove to now lead a godly and faultless life to the best of his ability and understanding. Every time he sinned, to demonstrate seriously his contrition and remorse, he would cut his toe with a razor and use the blood to write vows to God, all the while begging God's forgiveness. He knew little or nothing of the significance of Christ's death on the cross and how this could be made available to him freely by God's amazing grace, the freedom of forgiveness.

His thinking had been influenced by a book he had read which had been written by a highly esteemed, well known Coptic monk. By way of illustration, the monk had spoken of a long ladder by which many people laboriously climbed to reach heaven. At the very last step a struggler fell and was hell bound. The writer's application was that this illustrated the struggle of each person to reach heaven. One could strive the whole of life, but just before death commit a single sin, which meant heaven was forfeited and hell's embrace was the final destination after all.

Feyez, like many saints before him, was terrified at the thought. Was it really possible to pursue heaven through perfect living for the whole of one's life only to forfeit all hope and be consigned to hell because of a single sin at the end of it all? Confusion, frustration and anxiety gripped him. But with typical resolve he determined to find an answer to that ancient question: How does one please God and live in harmony with Him for eternity? In the meantime there were other duties for which he had accepted responsibility which called for his attention.

Youth Ministry

As a newly appointed youth leader, Feyez diligently organised programmes for meetings, speakers' schedules and weekly visits. His monthly programme had four emphases: Bible study, spiritual development, church history, rituals and traditions. If there was a fifth week in the month, this was given to debates, discussions and spoken presentations by members of the group. He urged his young charges to pursue Bible reading, prayer from the Agbia (hourly prayer book) and regular church attendance. He visited the members of his class every week. On Thursdays, the day of the youth meeting, he would hire a bicycle to revisit each home to remind each class member of the evening meeting. He was relentlessly persistent in pursuit of and care for his flock.

One recalcitrant, Nabil, sorely tested his patience. Each week Feyez faithfully visited Nabil to ask him to come to the meetings. Each week Nabil declined. After four months of repeatedly regular visits, Feyez was delighted when Nabil finally agreed to come. His thankfulness to God was short lived when Nabil confessed he had only agreed to come at his mother's suggestion as a means of reducing Feyez's pressure on him. Nabil never did accept the invitation to come to church or to God. Shortly afterwards he was apprehended while shoplifting. Duly imprisoned, his life continued in a downward spiral.

Preaching at last

In 1953 Feyez delivered his first sermon. It was at the weekly youth meeting. His topic was "Should we serve God in our youth or in our old age?" During the address he quoted John 21:18 in which Jesus was speaking to Peter, *"...When you were younger you dressed yourself and went where you wanted; but when you are old..."* At this point embarrassingly his mind froze and his memory went blank. All he could do was to repeat "but when you are old..." several times. Fr Boulos once more graciously stepped in to rescue his young friend.

In spite of Feyez's inadequacy, God used his youthful zeal to impact others greatly. Years later it was noted that from that youth group there came at least five priests, numerous monks and two bishops. Such are the rewards of faithfulness in the little things.

> **In spite of Feyez's inadvertency, God used his youthful zeal to impact others greatly ... which resulted in a revival within the Christian community in the city.**

Feyez was also impacted by the work of another man, Habib Girgius. He introduced the concept of Sunday school into the Coptic Church. He gathered and enthused tertiary students, training them and sending them forth to introduce the revelation of Sunday school wherever they went. One of his disciples was Fr Boulos who was sent on a mission to Damanhoor which resulted in a revival within the Christian community in the city.

Fr Boulos was one of the first "educated" priests within the modern Coptic Church. He'd had an encounter with Jesus. He was on fire for God. He was comparatively young when he came to St George's in Damanhoor. His enthusiasm for Christ and his church was contagious. He cared for the youth, attending and speaking at each of their meetings. His home was always open for any visitor. He was diligent in prayer. He preached the Word of God and encouraged his people to study the Bible. During summer vacations he initiated church clubs which bonded the youth together. He set up scripture memorisation competitions. Feyez won a special 'golden' Bible for memorising 500 verses in one of the competitions. Fr Boulos cared for the poor, supervising distribution of resources to meet their needs. He reached out to the unchurched by sending out his trained youth to distant villages to distribute Bibles and conduct Sunday school classes. And by the consistent example of his life, he made a permanent impression on the life of young Feyez.

Egyptian village life was comparatively primitive. There were no hotels, phones, street directories or churches. The young 'missionaries' sent out by Fr Boulos would find a Christian family in the village and use their home as a base for local operations. They would eat, drink and sleep in that home, just as Jesus' disciples had done, until it was time to move on.

Upon arriving in a village they would ask the whereabouts of 'George's' house. Not that they knew 'George'. It was known as a common name for Christians throughout Egypt. If there was none of that name, frequently a local might suggest that they might mean 'John'. This also was a common Christian name. Upon arrival at the Christian home the team would speak to the residents about God and give them a Bible. 'George' or 'John' would then take them to introduce them to other nominal Christians in the village.

With the onset of darkness the visiting missionaries would make to go to another village, fully aware that rules of hospitality required their contact to offer them overnight accommodation and food. When such an offer was inevitably made, it was always gratefully accepted. Before moving on, the host would also provide for them contacts and information regarding nearby villages. This annual four months summer activity was invaluable training for Feyez.

During the school year Fr Boulos encouraged the young missionaries to travel to closer villages each Friday to introduce the benefits of Sunday School to their churches. Teams of two walked through farms singing and worshipping God till they reached their destination. They felt they were literally reproducing the message and methods of Jesus.

Like any innovation, Sunday school was not immediately welcomed into every church. Some priests and church leaders saw it as a threat to their authority, particularly if they personally had less education than the student enthusiasts. They dealt with the intruders by branding them as 'Protestants', a poison chalice of heresy of the worst order within the conservative Coptic community.

At the village of El Mahmoodia, when Feyez and his co-worker gathered the children for mass and a Bible lesson, after the liturgy, the local priest instructed the church cleaner to remove the intruders from the premises immediately. The young workers repaired to the steps outside the church. Feyez stood teaching songs to the children with his back to the next-door apartments in which the priest lived. Suddenly, to the amusement of the children and the momentary surprise of Feyez, he found himself bucketed with filthy water, chicken intestines and feathers. The parish priest was serious about their leaving the church premises. To encourage this, he had tipped the foul contents of his waste bucket over Feyez from his second floor balcony. Ever persistent, Feyez simply removed the grosser bits from his person and continued leading the children in singing as if nothing had happened. This would not be the last time that Feyez, in pursuit of a more noble cause, would exasperate church authorities.

University

1951 was a critical year for young Feyez. It was his all important final year of secondary school. To be accepted into the Faculty of Medicine, as he hoped, he would need to excel at his final secondary school exam. Unfortunately his father Henien was diagnosed with cancer. The family used all their savings taking him from one hospital to another, from one medical specialist to another, in a vain desperate attempt to find a cure. It was all to no avail. Henien died aged 49 years. When the family's sole breadwinner died, with him went Feyez's hope for funding an expensive medical degree - if he could have qualified.

Further troubles beset the young man as crises leading to revolution rocked the nation. Schools and other facilities were virtually closed throughout the year. Not surprisingly Feyez did not obtain the marks needed in his end of school exams, to gain admission to study medicine. He opted for Law instead.

After queuing for a long time to hand in his application, when he finally fronted at the registrar's desk, he experienced discrimination common to Christians in Muslim Egypt. The registrar refused even to take his application.

With doors to the study of Medicine and Law firmly closed, he enrolled in a Bachelor of Arts majoring in English. But two years later when Gamel Abdul Nasser assumed the presidency, in a burst on Nationalism, he short-sightedly banned the teaching of English. Feyez was obliged to change courses to major in history and archaeology instead.

By Feyez's second year at University, family finances were in a critical state. There was little or no income and debts were mounting up. To support the family, Feyez decided to sit for an examination which could lead to his winning an appointment as a school teacher. For three months he studied hard for the examinable subjects: Arabic, English, Mathematics, Teaching and Learning Methodologies. Among three thousand examinees, Feyez came fourteenth. He won a position to teach at Lakana Shobra Kheet, 24 kilometres distant from Damanhoor where the family lived. Here he taught for two years before being transferred for three years to Ameriah and Taawen schools in Damanhoor.

While at Lakana, Feyez taught each morning, then hastened back to Damanhoor to catch the train to Alexandria to arrive in time for afternoon lectures at the University. Friends loaned him their notes of the missed morning lectures. Zakaria Yousef was one such who became a friend for life.

On the hour's train ride back to Damanhoor and during each evening, Feyez transcribed the lecture notes and studied. His monthly teaching salary was fifteen Egyptian pounds, all of which went on transport costs and support of his family.

Following graduation, Feyez applied for a position as a fully licensed teacher with the Ministry of Education in Cairo. For this he needed to complete successfully an interview process. He was advised of the date by letter. A week before the appointed day, an acquaintance asked why he had not attended the Education Department's interview for that day. Apparently the date had been advanced a week, but in that he lived outside Cairo, he had not received advice of it. He left immediately and caught a train for Cairo.

Arriving at the interview venue after 5 p.m., the only person still on the premises was the cleaner, who confirmed that the interviews had indeed been held on that very day but that they were now all completed. Then the cleaner identified a man walking nearby as president of the interview committee. Running to catch up with him, Feyez explained the predicament in which he inadvertently found himself. Sympathetic to his plight, the president agreed to arrange a special interview for him the next morning.

Upon arrival Feyez was confronted with a panel of three interviewers, who firstly tried to intimidate and humiliate him by asking his mother's name. This is culturally unacceptable and quite inappropriate within the Egyptian context. Feyez parried the thrust by deftly replying, "Her name is Egypt - sir!"

The panel was duly impressed. After successfully negotiating further questions, he was later advised he was appointed to teach history and geography at Ameriah in Damanhoor.

In Government and Church Service

Despite the pressures of teaching, studying and travel, Feyez never wavered from his commitment to leadership of the youth ministry, organising and participating in extensive summer activities, attendance at Church and more frequently preaching at Friday church services. Fr Boulos often invited well-known outside speakers to conduct revival meetings in the church. One of the most influential was Archdeacon Obade Mikhail.

He spoke with such passion and power often loudly rebuking his hearers with spiritual authority. To tobacco smokers he would say, "Brothers, you who inhale with your mouth and exhale through your nose, if God wanted you to be a chimney, he would have designed an opening in the top of your head!"

If any of the congregation complained about the volume of his sermons he would reply, "If you saw that your son was about to be crushed by an onrushing train, would you quietly whisper to him to move out of the way, or would you yell at the top of your lungs? I see people in danger of imminent death and hell. The urgency of their plight grips me. I must yell to warn them."

Young Feyez was very impressed with Obade's style and content. Not unsurprisingly he wanted to be just like him.

Church and its associated activities absorbed increasing amounts of Feyez's time. St George's was unique in that it was the only church which permitted non-traditional, nonreligious activities on its premises at that time. Feyez became involved in theatre, cycling excursions, wrestling tournaments and sundry other activities. Often there were unexpected dramatic outcomes.

During a dress rehearsal for the 1957 Christmas play, a little boy grabbed a branch of an artificial Christmas tree. He was unable to let go. Because of faulty wiring the branch was 'live' with 240 volt electricity. Feyez, with no thought for his own safety, instinctively raced to rescue the boy. As he reached out he also was held by the current, unable to release himself or the boy. Fortunately an engineer was present who had a better knowledge of the properties of electricity. He ran to the switchboard and disconnected the appropriate circuit, thus saving the boy and Feyez. However the shock of this event in no way deterred Feyez's love of drama.

In another Christmas play he was assigned the role of John the Baptist. Kamal Abadeer, a professional writer, producer and director, in one scene was to play opposite him in the role of King Herod. At one point Kamal, forgetting his scripted lines, improvised. Feyez not to be outdone replied in kind. Much for the enjoyment of the crowd, the unscripted verbal jousting continued for 30 minutes till the stage manager brought down the curtain.

Without his realising it, Feyez's flexibility, disciplined study patterns, strong work ethic, extended involvement in church activities and developing preaching skills, were about to launch him into a drama of a different order.

CHAPTER 2

THE CALL

In December 1958, Fr Boulos sent Feyez on a preaching assignment which he himself had declined. It was in the city of Shebeen El Kom, 100 kms south of Damanhoor. Unbeknown to Feyez, Fr Boulos was providing practical training for a future which Feyez hadn't even considered.

At Shebeen El Kom, Feyez preached on 'The Elements of a Prosperous Ministry'. He said that effective ministry results from cooperation between priest and people. By way of illustration he sketched a word picture of a priest trying to drive a car uphill. Just as the priest seemed almost to succeed, the car would roll back down the hill. He struggled again and again until his watching congregation came to his rescue. They got behind the car and prevented its backward roll. The lesson was obvious. Spiritual leadership needs to be undergirded by prayer, fasting and participation of all of the people.

Fr Boulos obviously received a favourable report of the young preacher's message, because within a week he sent a deacon with a letter requesting Feyez to report to the church forthwith and be ready to deliver another sermon. This was short notice indeed. But Feyez rose to the challenge and obviously impressed those who had been invited to be present. These included a high-ranking Bishop, Metropolitan Benjamin and many of the deacons from Shebeen El Kom.

After the service, Metropolitan Benjamin asked Feyez if he could read the Coptic language. This was important because it was and is the official liturgical language of the Orthodox Church in Egypt. Satisfied with Feyez's ability in this crucial area, the Metropolitan next enquired whether or not Feyez would consider training to become a priest. Feyez's immediate response was that he would consider it an honour, if that was God's will for him. Metropolitan Benjamin obviously concluded that was all he needed to hear. He instructed Fr Boulos to make the preparatory arrangements, to inform Feyez's family and to find a wife for him!

Fr Boulos was faced with a dilemma. How could he inform Feyez's family of the Metropolitan's decision? He decided to wait until the next Feast Day of the church. With festivities in full swing, he told the family that God had called Feyez to become a priest of the congregation of Shebeen El Kom. Merriment suddenly became mourning. Even the specially prepared food lost its taste and was later thrown out, uneaten.

When Feyez's mother heard the news, she was distraught. Feyez had been the sole income earner for the whole family. He was also surrogate disciplinarian for his younger siblings. Who would hunt for the young Maurice during his frequent truancies? How would the family get on without him? How could it survive penury on the pittance of a novice priest's allowance?

Throughout January 1959, Feyez went to bed each night and tried to sleep while his mother spent the whole night next to him sobbing and wailing in her distress. He felt trapped between his duty to respond to God's call given him by his local priest and the Metropolitan, and his filial responsibilities to his mother and other family members. He could not resolve these seemingly irreconcilable tensions, till one night the Lord spoke to him through a dream.

In the dream, Jesus appeared to be sitting on top of a high pillar above an unfamiliar bridge. He was dressed in flowing robes similar to those which priests wore. From him emanated awesome majesty appropriate to his person. As Feyez approached the bridge, Jesus lowered a censor for him, similar to those used by priests performing liturgical functions in Coptic church services. For Feyez this confirmed that the call to priestly office was indeed from God for him. That left only the not insignificant problem of overcoming the family's reluctance.

Not long afterwards, older brother Phillip, who was not particularly religious, also had an unusual dream. In his dream, their deceased father stood beside Phillip and told him to leave Feyez alone and not stand in his way any longer. Phillip awoke terrified and ran to his mother's room. For once she was asleep. The boy woke her and reported what had happened. She in turn woke Feyez and gave him permission to go ahead and do what he felt was right.

Marriage

With these obstacles removed, the next, finding a wife, was a comparatively minor matter! His mother suggested a distant relative named Violet could be suitable. She worked in a public water utility in Alexandria and was somewhat surprised, when unannounced, Feyez paid her a visit at work on January 28 1959. He did this only after receiving approval and permission from Violet's mother.

They had not previously known each other personally. Violet knew of Feyez only through his church activities. Feyez asked if she could take the rest of the day off as Fr Boulos needed to see her to discuss a matter of great importance. Violet regarded Fr Boulos so highly that just the mention of his name ensured her compliance.

As if to emphasise the gravity of the situation, Feyez uncharacteristically hired a taxi to whisk them to Damanhoor, an hour's drive distant. During the drive, Feyez revealed that God had called him to the priesthood and that he was to be appointed to the church in Shebeen El Kom. Consequently he needed a marriage partner. Would Violet consent to being his wife?

Violet was not particularly interested in marriage. She had been deeply impressed by the life led by her cousin Omena Hena, who had resigned her position as a school teacher to become a nun. A room in Omena's house was dedicated for worship. She also made clothes for the poor and shared her own food with them.

A week previously, her name, as well as names of several women who had been proposed as a suitable wife had been placed on her church's altar. At the end of the seventh church service after the placement, the piece of paper on which her name was written, was selected by a young boy. This was interpreted as revealing God's will for her that she was to marry Feyez. This practice is highly regarded within the Coptic Church. The same procedure is followed in the final selection process of its Popes.

Feyez's marriage proposal simultaneously shocked and delighted Violet. To receive a proposal to marry someone who was destined for the priesthood was considered a great honour. That it should have come from Feyez was additionally pleasing, because of his good reputation as an esteemed servant of the church. As an obedient daughter she would not disappoint her family who would undoubtedly approve such a union. Besides, in Egyptian culture, marrying a relative made it safe. Not surprisingly therefore, as the taxi took her toward her appointment with destiny, she sensed God saying to her, "You wanted to serve me. Here is the way you can do so."

As for Feyez, he knew Violet's family well. He was very impressed with her reputation for godliness and upright living. Marriage was seen as a prerequisite for entering his holy vocation. Normally adults were engaged to be married for 1 to 2 years before the actual event. In this case the priesthood beckoned and no delay could be entertained.

Once Violet's family had given their blessing, the engagement ring was purchased and the couple were formally engaged the next day. Two days later they were married.

In Western culture, men tend to marry the woman they love. In Egyptian Christian culture of the time and still in many cultures today, men love the woman they marry. One starts with a burst of emotion which is hopefully followed by commitment of the will. The other commences with commitment of the will followed by a blooming of the emotions. Either way works if God is central to each.

On February 1 1959, St George's church in Damanhoor was packed with people attending the wedding at which Metropolitan Benjamin officiated. Feyez would be the first priest resulting from the ministry of Fr Boulos. He would also be the fifth priest involved in the "revolutionary" Sunday school movement.

Following the ceremony, the newlyweds enjoyed a one night honeymoon in an apartment in Kafer El Dawar, after which Violet's brother Phillip, brought them back to the family home to continue the celebrations in time-honoured Egyptian fashion!

Ordination

One week later, all the family travelled to Shebeen El Kom for Feyez's ordination and induction as priest of the local congregation. Again the church was crowded beyond capacity. Well wishers had come from many distant parts of Egypt to celebrate the event. Fr Makarry (later to become Bishop Samuel), Fr Shenouda (later Bishop Youhannes of Tanta), Fr Iskander and many other well-known notables were in attendance.

During a Coptic Church ordination ceremony, it is customary for the presiding Bishop to blow onto the face of the new priest and say, "Receive a spirit from my spirit." This is said to symbolise the actions of Moses, when he appointed 70 elders to whom he was to delegate some leadership responsibilities (Numbers 11:16-17). When the Metropolitan blew on Feyez, the young priest sensed an extraordinary surge of heat throughout his whole body. This would only make sense to him when years later, he learned of the activities of the Holy Spirit about which at this time he knew nothing.

At the time of ordination, Coptic priests take a new name. Feyez had chosen the name Samuel, but the Metropolitan named him Zakaria. In Coptic Church history, Zakaria was the name of a young monk, who so impressed the Coptic Pope when they met, that the Pope requested the monk to pray for him so that the Pope might be as Spirit-filled as was obviously the young monk. Metropolitan Benjamin was similarly impressed by the young charge who stood before him on that day and wished this new Zakaria to start from where the old Feyez ended.

Father Zakaria, true to his ancient namesake, adopted Zechariah 4: 6 as his life's motto: *"... Not by might nor by power, but by my Spirit, says the Lord Almighty."*

After the ordination ceremony there came the celebrations and festivities. Fr Makarry, Fr Boulos and other distinguished guests addressed the crowd, at the end of which an old priest, Fr Anthony Ibrahim, rose to add his wisdom.

"Many people have stood to congratulate you, but I stand to console you," he said. The crowd murmured their displeasure at these words which seemed at variance with the celebratory atmosphere of the occasion up to now. But Father Anthony would not be sidetracked. He solemnly continued, "I am referring to God's realistic advice to all who embrace the ministry. God said that if you offer yourself for ministry, you need to prepare for trials. Many today have talked about the honour, but none have mentioned the tribulations. Fr Zakaria, prepare to carry your cross."

With the knowledge of what later happened, it would have to be agreed that on that day, Fr Anthony was speaking with rare, accurate prophetic insight.

After one week and one day of the joys of marriage, it all ended for Zakaria, for the time being. He had to travel to Cairo to spend the next 40 days in seclusion to prepare for his new vocation of ministry. This is a mandatory practice for all newly appointed priests of the Coptic Church. His new wife stayed behind in Damanhoor to prepare for her new life as wife of the parish priest in Shebeen El Kom. When Zakaria returned to Damanhoor, he hired a car to transport the furniture his wife purchased for their first home together.

A New Home

This would not be an easy transition for Violet. For her it would be the first time she had left the shelter of the closely knit family in which she had been nurtured. Now she had to launch out into a totally different life, one of responsibility and service to others. She knew little about housekeeping and even less about budgeting. Her husband was even less knowledgeable regarding domestic management. There was hardly enough money to buy food. Clothes for Violet were occasionally provided by her family.

Metropolitan Benjamin was an excellent pastor to his new priest and his wife. He needed to be. Violet's mother had sternly warned him that the young ones were now his responsibility. Undoubtedly she would hold him accountable for whatever happened to them. But he also was unaware of the couple's continuing desperate financial straits.

Of the monthly salary of 15 Egyptian pounds, 5 paid the rent, 5 were still sent home as family support and 5 remained, which was all they had to meet their daily needs. Often they survived on no more than bread sprinkled with salt. To make it more bearable, they'd joke with each other about why neither of them could find any meat in their bowls. Fortunately there were no additional mouths to feed in the form of children - yet.

If finances were not already tight enough, matters worsened by Zakaria's tendency to value food for the brain as being more important than that for the stomach. Frequently he would take the housekeeping money to buy books, which left them eating nothing but stale bread for the rest of the month.

Their financial and dietary problems were compounded further by Zakaria's habit of extending hospitality to all and sundry. With little or no money to feed themselves, let alone their guests, Violet often repaired to the local jeweller's shop to get the best price she could, for yet another gold wedding present she had received. Eventually she sold all the gold she possessed just to buy basic necessities of food, a fact she never divulged to her husband till many years later. She hadn't wanted to worry him unnecessarily.

A Novice in Ministry

Ministry commenced on a memorably difficult note for Zakaria. The senior priest in charge of the church left him to conduct his first full service unaided. The complex liturgy of the Coptic Church normally lasts for approximately 2 1/2 hours and involves numerous rituals, hymns, readings and Holy Communion.

During Zakaria's first service, he sang the tunes very slowly as he had been taught in his 40 days of preparation in Cairo. The problem was, he extended the tunes in many different directions while he tried to work out how each should finish. Instead of a 2 1/2 hour service, the mass dragged on for 6 hours! Violet's brother Phillip's exasperation probably reflected that of many. He commented, "You almost caused me to deny Christ!"

After laughing it off as a good learning experience, Zakaria enthusiastically pursued his new vocation. Now he could serve people and be saved from hell. Or at least that's what he thought. To avoid consignment to the nether regions for eternity was always something which had troubled him. At last he felt relieved of that anxiety, because he had formed the view that God would never cast a priest into hell, because that would cause public humiliation and bring dishonour onto God himself.

Zakaria and Violet immersed themselves in the ministry, attending meetings, visiting the sick and elderly in their homes and praying with all who had a need.

In January 1960 their first child, Janet was born. Metropolitan Benjamin was as excited as the new parents, phoning them daily to enquire after their welfare. The members of the church were not quite of the same mind. When with the aid of a cousin Victoria, Violet brought a pram for the baby for 3 Egyptian pounds, some in the congregation grumbled at the "high life" of the young priest's family. The pram was returned to the place from which it was purchased.

Searching for Salvation

Although peace was restored in the church it wasn't to remain so in Zakaria's mind. His sense of security was shattered by the innocent humour of the Maaleem, that is, the head deacon, one Mouneer by name.

One day Maaleem Mouneer jested with Zakaria about a deacon, who to his surprise after death, ended up in hell. To his horror the deacon next noticed that he had been preceded by the head deacon. The head deacon hushed him to be quiet because their priest was nearby as well.

Maaleem Mouneer expected Fr Zakaria to burst into simultaneous spontaneous laughter with him. Instead, he only stared in paled silence. He'd been relying on his elevation to the priesthood as a guarantee for his salvation. Now his security had been shattered by an innocent joke. He resolved from that day on to research the concept of salvation, until he could be certain of the divine process and its outcomes.

Zakaria read every book on salvation that he could find at the time. He even read the book, *How to be Saved* by the 19th century American evangelist, D. L. Moody. Each of the books spoke very precisely about the nature and consequences of sin. To this he could readily relate. But unfortunately they had far less to say about salvation. Each seemed to reduce it to a formula of just believing on Jesus. Surely this approach was far too simplistic. There had to be more required than this.

Later Zakaria concluded that the issue was so simply stated, because each of the writers was perhaps addressing a Muslim readership.

The question of just how could he and his people be really saved and be acceptable to God, burned persistently deep within him. Unanswered to his satisfaction it would not be quenched.

Regardless of the unresolved matter of salvation, Zakaria energetically hurled himself into local ministry, leading services, Bible studies, prayer meetings and daily visitation. There were 500 members in the congregation and Zakaria was determined to be a father in the faith to each and every one of them. He was constantly encouraging people to live by the teachings of the holy book, the Bible, to pray and attend church regularly.

To assist him to prepare to lead a special Bible study for half a dozen well educated families, he purchased a set of Matthew Henry's Bible commentaries. From these he would read and select the portions relevant to Coptic Orthodox belief. The church had no tradition of verse by verse exposition of the Bible. In reading the Bible, he thought one had to be wary of the cunning inclusion of modern heresies into the text. Zakaria highlighted Ephesians 2: 8 – 9, which says one is saved by grace not by works. He noted in the margin in thick red ink that these verses were probably 'Protestant verses' inserted in the translation to promote their own beliefs.

As his scholarship increased through his voracious reading habits, he started to systematise his knowledge in a series of booklets to instruct those beyond his immediate pastoral care. *The History of the Division between the Churches* and *The Heresy of Preparing Spirits* were among the first titles of this period. He also wrote the first of his apologetic books for Muslim readers, defending the doctrines of the Trinity (using the Quran) and the deity of Jesus.

Pastors and priests often joke that church would be a wonderful place if only there were no people! This is because in almost every congregation, there are usually to be found some difficult individuals who make life troublesome for others, by their domineering aspirations or their widely expressed contrary opinions. The congregation at Shebeen El Kom was no exception.

A teacher from the local agricultural institute from an affluent family, tried to dominate the ministry of the church, by repeatedly publicly insulting the ministry in general and Zakaria in particular. Unable to resolve the conflict, Zakaria petitioned Metropolitan Benjamin to remove his adversary's involvement in ministry aspects of the church life and confine him to administrative and financial responsibilities. Like many other church authorities before him, confronted with alienating a longstanding financial contributor or distressing a young priest, Metropolitan Benjamin opted to placate the congregant. Zakaria would be transferred elsewhere.

By this time Zakaria's energy, enthusiasm and effectiveness were known beyond where he served. Metropolitan Isaac, Bishop of Tanta, a nearby diocese, was delighted to accept his services.

Again the family was on the move. But by this time it had grown to include three young children, Janet born in 1960, Feyez born in 1961 and Benjamin born in 1963. The last was so named to honour the kind and loving Metropolitan Benjamin, who had up till that time cared for them so well.

CHAPTER 3

GOD STEPS IN

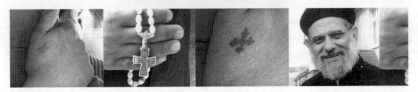

Dancing with Wolves

Metropolitan Benjamin accompanied Zakaria to his new church, St Mary's in the suburb of El Sagha in the city of Tanta. Of the four Coptic churches in Tanta, St Mary's was the oldest. It was strategically located near El Saied El Badawy, the largest mosque in the province. Here God would work his greatest transformation to date in the life and ministry of his servant.

Zakaria was already well known in the city. He was one of the few priests at that time with any education of note. He was also well known for his well modulated voice and the dramatic delivery of his sermons. He was becoming a much sought-after speaker among Orthodox congregations.

Soon after Zakaria commenced his ministry in Tanta, another group of newcomers also arrived. It was Khalas El Nefoos, 'Salvation Of Souls', a much maligned Protestant organization, which was dreaded by the Coptic Orthodox church. They already had congregations in other cities. Wherever they went they were attacked by the Orthodox, because they epitomised those twin fears of the church which had threatened its existence from its very beginning 20 centuries earlier - heresy and schism.

Some of the earnest people from 'Salvation Of Souls' in their zeal to spread their understanding of truth, targeted the Coptic congregations. They handed out notices advertising an evening meeting. Seeking to deflect this territorial encroachment, an Orthodox priest warned his people that, "A disastrous thing has come our way; the prowling wolves have arrived in Tanta and are inviting people to their meeting tonight."

Instead of frightening off the faithful, the priest's dramatic announcement only aroused their curiosity. The building in which the meeting was held was jammed with Orthodox people, eager to see for themselves the wolverine messengers who would visit disaster on their unsuspecting city. The message, 'St Mary - My Soul Exalts the Lord', was conceptualised well to be acceptable to Orthodox sentiments.

The crowd was pleasantly surprised and impressed. These 'wolves' didn't seem to be too dangerous. Some decided to attend further meetings to learn more. Concerns for their flocks were raised by Coptic shepherds among themselves who referred the matter to their Bishop.

To guard against what they considered to be false teaching, not to mention pilfering of their people, priests across the city preached against 'Salvation of Souls'. To confront the crisis a different strategy was developed. The hierarchy, after due consideration, under the direction of Metropolitan Isaac decided to appoint their most popular preacher, Zakaria, to rebut the nascent heresy infecting their congregations via 'Salvation Of Souls'. This inoculation would certainly return all Orthodox parishioners to the fold of the one true Church. Peace and tranquillity, as before, would not be far off – or so they thought.

Meticulous Research

Zakaria planned his strategy carefully. He decided he would smash the lies with truth. Instead of preaching against 'Salvation Of Souls', he would preach the unarguably correct doctrines as developed within the Orthodox Church from its beginnings. This would surely expose the wilful falsity of these Protestant devils. All would come back to mother Church. The crisis would be resolved. The hierarchy could get on with whatever they did gainfully to pass their days and simple priests like him, could once more return to pastoring their flocks undisturbed.

But to implement his strategy, Zakaria determined that he first needed to do a little more study of the topic at hand, to make sure his arguments were impregnable.

Toward the end of 1963, Zakaria discovered the library of the El Syrian Monastery in Wadi El Natroon. He found a treasure trove of hundreds of books relating to the Orthodox position on the subject of salvation. These went all the way back to the fourth century Nicene Fathers. Zakaria was ecstatic at the prospect of mining such a rich vein of truth.

A temporary setback was encountered when the monastic order's librarian advised that the precious volumes could not be removed from the library, because these were the only copies in the whole of Egypt in which were documented the authentic sayings of the early Church Fathers. The only other possibility was to obtain another set from abroad. Then Zakaria could study the matter at leisure in his own home.

This however would present two additional obstacles. Firstly, importation of books could only be done legally through government channels. They exclusively inspected all such import items and withheld whatever was contrary to the government's official (religious) position. Even if the officials never confiscated the books, it would still take even the world's most efficient customs officers, years to peruse carefully the whole thirty-eight volumes. Egyptian officialdom was hardly renowned for the speed with which they dealt with any matter, unless perhaps monetary encouragement could oil bureaucratic wheels to turn a little faster.

The second obstacle was that local currency to the value of US$20 was the maximum permitted for exchange or foreign purchase matters. 38 volumes would certainly cost somewhat more than $20.

As Zakaria pondered his dilemma, during one of his weekly visits to those who had been admitted for treatment to the American hospital in

Tanta, that institution's manager innocently offered his help should any need arise and if he could use his office to assist in any way. Zakaria didn't need a second invitation. He leapt at the opportunity.

He told the manager of his desperation to import a certain book from the USA and of his inability to import it on his own authority. Could the manager perhaps possibly organise it for him and have it included in his next shipment of medicines to the hospital? It might be argued that there was a tenuous link to legality. After all, the book would be medicine at least for Zakaria's soul.

The manager duly noted all particulars and promised to do his best. However three weeks later the hospital manager contacted Zakaria in a slightly alarmed state. "Did you ask for a book or a series of books? It seems that what you seek consists of thirty-eight volumes!" he said.

Zakaria calmly responded that it was actually the 38 volumes in which he was interested. The manager, somewhat exasperated, explained that while he was prepared to buy one book and present it as a gift to the good Father, 38 was somewhat more than he had in mind. Zakaria assured him that there was no way one could expect such magnanimity. Besides, he fully intended to pay for all the books himself. Within a month the books arrived. A loan from a savings cooperative saved the day, if not the family's diet.

Once the books arrived, the well ordered Botross family schedule changed dramatically. Zakaria asked his colleague, Fr Youhanna, to accept full responsibility for all church activities except for one service a week which he would continue to conduct. To avoid interruption, he had the phone disconnected. He withdrew from his family, shutting himself in his study, to which his meals were delivered. For 16 hours a day he devoured the writings of the early Fathers, tracing every reference regarding the topic of salvation, through every one of the 38 volumes.

Eventually he happened upon a Good Friday sermon of the famous Cyril of Jerusalem delivered in the fourth century. It was based upon Jesus assuring a penitent criminal of salvation, as both died on their respective crosses (Luke 23:32-43).

The message of the great trustworthy Orthodox St Cyril of Jerusalem, spoke powerfully across the centuries to the diligently seeking Zakaria of Tanta in Egypt. When Zakaria for the first time fully realised the enormity of just what Jesus had done and achieved for him personally when he offered himself as a ransom for everyone's sin on the cross, he fell to his knees amazed. At last he understood the stunning simplicity of God's plan for salvation.

Through the sacrifice of the sinless Jesus, who willingly died in the place of all who would trust in what he had done, he, Zakaria could be freed of the awful guilt and burdensome anxiety which had bedevilled him all these years. Salvation was not something he could earn, no matter how hard he tried. It was something which God freely offered, to any who confessed and turned away from their sin and believed on and trusted in Jesus. It was that simple.

Saved at Last

On his knees Zakaria wept. He prayed. He laughed. All the study he had done, all the verses of Scripture he had read, it made sense at last. Now he knew not just some dry doctrine. He experienced the reality behind that doctrine. No longer was he just another professional purveyor of religion. He was a believer, a child of God, adopted into His family. Through Jesus he had obtained personal forgiveness. He was reconciled with God at last. Jesus was his leader, his treasure, his all in all.

Zakaria continued to research the concept of salvation, but from now on from the perspective of an insider, one who understood and was being transformed. Eventually he was ready for his public defence. Having prepared a series of sermons on the topic of salvation from the Orthodox perspective, he announced that weekly "revival" meetings would be held each Friday afternoon and evening.

But then God confronted him with another challenge for his curious mind and hungry spirit.

In the course of preparing for his sermon series, Zakaria had read that when the early Church Father, John Chrysostom preached, listeners wept under conviction for their sins. Zakaria wondered why and how this could happen. At about the same time he read a book by Fr Matta

El Meskeen entitled, *The Holy Spirit in People's Lives.* Fr Matta had been God's agent of spiritual renewal in modern monastic Coptic life. Zakaria knew and respected him greatly. Matta spoke of the necessity of being filled with the Holy Spirit to be able to minister to others effectively.

Zakaria noted the similarities between Matta's teaching and Jesus' instruction to his disciples. His followers were not to depart from Jerusalem until they also were clothed with the Holy Spirit's power to enable them to minister effectively. Zakaria became convinced that the same principle should apply in his case as well.

Three days prior to his first "revival" meeting, Zakaria began to fast and seek God for his own special anointing by the Holy Spirit. Repeatedly he begged God to hasten the Spirit's anointing upon him. On the third day he went to the church and shut himself in an upstairs room prior to the meeting. As he continued to pray fervently, he resolved not to descend to the service until he was truly filled with the Holy Spirit. On his knees, he begged God to grant his petition.

Anointed for Ministry

His prayer was interrupted as he sensed God was asking him why he wanted to be filled. "Because I want people to be touched and saved" was his reply.

"Do you want them to be saved so that you can be called a great preacher?" the voice enquired.

"Oh God, do you think this is going to be for my self glorification?" Zakaria moaned. Heaviness seemed to descend upon him as if all his natural fiery zeal had been extinguished. Having locked the room's door, he slouched into a chair in a state of deep sadness and despair. The decision was made. He would not go downstairs to preach.

Back came the voice, "Why aren't you going down to preach? The people are waiting for you."

"If it is going to be just another sermon," Zakaria replied, "then Fr Youhanna may as well preach." In the ensuing heavy silence, minutes dragged by like years. Suddenly the voice returned, "Why do you want to be filled?"

"So that people can be saved from their sins and ungodly living," Zakaria repeated.

The voice asked just one last question.

"Do you seriously think that I can save your people from their sins and cannot save you from your ego?" Zakaria fell to his knees one more time with hope reborn.

"Lord empty me, take over, hide me and have all the glory" he prayed. Then he saw a vision of a large crowd of people trying to climb a mountain. In their eagerness to get to the summit they pushed and shoved one another. The other side of the mountain was sheer cliff. People having reached the top were still pushing, so that those in front of them fell over the cliff to their death.

In anguish Zakaria cried out, "Lord have mercy. Lord save, save, please save them!"

At that moment, something akin to a charge of electricity seemed to surge through Zakaria's body, the strength of which he'd never experienced before. His 'upper room' experience was suddenly interrupted by fierce knocking on his door. Unlocking it, Zakaria was confronted by two anxious church leaders who were about to smash the door down.

"Is everything okay?" they shouted somewhat panicked. They had been knocking for over 20 minutes. Zakaria had been oblivious to their noisy entreaties.

Duly reassured and composed, the little group went downstairs to where the crowd had been patiently waiting. Then Zakaria realised he'd forgotten to bring his sermon notes. That oversight was an opportunity for the Spirit to take over.

While the content of the message has been forgotten, its impact hasn't. Zakaria spoke. People and preacher began to weep uncontrollably. When the meeting finally concluded, people lingered within the church for hours, crying, praying and repenting. For the first time in the modern era, people in the Coptic Church heard the Gospel preached as understood by the early Church Fathers. With the layers of extraneous teachings of the centuries stripped away, there was the truth, as first delivered to the saints, in all its simplicity and awesome power. Revival broke out as the Holy Spirit visited Tanta.

Revival

From 1964 to 1966 Zakaria preached his series on salvation, justification, regeneration, sanctification and the infilling of the Holy Spirit. This was revolutionary. Never before in the history of Egyptian Coptic Orthodoxy had such words been uttered. People crowded into the weekly Friday morning meetings. Even 'Salvation of Souls' shut down their own meetings and came with their people to those in the Orthodox Church! The Orthodox objectives were being achieved, but not in a way they could ever have anticipated.

As the Lord continued to visit Tanta, people flocked to hear the ancient message of salvation. They became hungry for more of the Word of God.

They prayed, wept and repented in increasing numbers. They gave up their old ways. They were released and healed of the addictive habits of nicotine, alcohol and other drugs. Hymn singing wafted from homes. People praising God was heard in the streets. They gathered daily in homes, to study the Bible, sing hymns and pray fervently.

Zakaria was on fire. Every night he visited a different home to encourage and instruct the people. Attendance at the meetings at which he spoke continued to grow. People were receiving Christ and being filled by the Spirit all over the place. Typical was what happened to Shafeek Mina.

One evening he visited Zakaria at home and asked for prayer to be filled with the Holy Spirit. Together they prayed and believed God, but nothing appeared to happen. Then as Shafeek walked down the stairs to leave the apartment block, he sensed he was surrounded by a cloud. His vision seemed to blur. Fumblingly he found his way out of the building and stumbled home, all the while surrounded by a 'cloud'. All night he prayed.

Early in the morning he returned to Zakaria's apartment for more prayer. Soon afterwards, it became his custom to seek out nearby unreached villages to share the good news with them. When in Tanta, he would walk the streets listening for the sound of hymns. Whenever he found such a home, he would knock on the door and ask permission from those inside, for him to join in their worship.

News of the revival spread fast. Zakaria started to receive speaking invitations from towns and cities across Egypt. From Alexandria in the North to Aswan in the South, whenever Zakaria spoke people responded and the revival gained pace. To encourage, strengthen and instruct those who responded, Zakaria wrote, collated and posted fortnightly follow-up materials to as many as possible of those who were responding. In this way he provided basic biblical teaching on the Bible, prayer, praise, justification, salvation, the Holy Spirit and sanctification.

News of the revival spread fast. Zakaria started to receive speaking invitations from towns and cities across Egypt.

These subjects were somewhat novel within contemporary Egyptian Orthodox tradition. The results spoke for themselves. People were responding, repenting and growing in their newfound faith and their desire to follow Jesus unreservedly.

Not everyone responded immediately in the most desired or hoped for way. At the revival meetings at Kafer El Dawar, people 'repenting' of their addiction to nicotine, used to throw away their packs of cigarettes immediately. Four decades later, one attendee recalled that at that time his response was to collect all the thrown away discarded packs and add them to his personal supply of cigarettes. There are many unplanned blessings which flow from a person's salvation, but this was not meant to be one of them.

Repentance from sin, salvations, a hunger for the Bible's teaching, increased prayer, praise and worship, were not the only evidences of the Holy Spirit's presence and operations. In Tanta, one day as Zakaria arrived at the church, he found the church cleaner's son uncontrollably rolling around on the ground. The boy's father said his son was demonically oppressed.

Healings and Deliverance

Zakaria had confronted this phenomenon previously, without success at Shebeen El Kom. This time the outcome would be different. When Zakaria took the young boy into the church and prayed over him, immediately a demon cried out, "I'll get out! I'll get out!" Subsequently the young boy got up, embraced Zakaria and testified to all present how differently he felt. Not unsurprisingly his father was delighted. In such situations, news travelled from one to the other almost at Internet speed.

People afflicted by demonic influences flocked to Zakaria to have him pray for them. They also brought their friends and relatives for prayer. Without exception, none departed disappointed. All were released, healed and went on their way praising God.

Even Muslim farmers who attended a nearby mosque came. Having turned up, they said they wanted to turn away from satanic captivity and be freed by prayer in Jesus' name. After casting out demons from each, Zakaria carefully explained the gospel in simple terms appropriate to the farmers' understanding. Many believed on Jesus, prayed to receive the Holy Spirit and were baptised.

One Friday morning a lady approached Zakaria and asked him to pray for her deliverance. He did and she was. Then the next Sunday another lady came with her mother and aunt with the same request. As Zakaria started to pray, a somewhat familiar demonic voice called out, "We were here on Friday." Zakaria realised that the lady was the same person for whom he had prayed on the previous Friday, who on that occasion had disguised herself as a farm girl. In fact she was a schoolteacher. The demons were in the habit of tormenting and humiliating her, by compelling her to roll on the classroom floor in front of her students.

Zakaria asked the demons how they had re-entered the lady after being cast out just two days previously. "Ask the mother and aunt," they replied. When these two ladies denied any knowledge of what had happened, immediately the demons shouted, "Liars! Liars!"

Zakaria ordered the demons to remain silent, to release the girl's mind and allow her to speak for herself. The girl then explained that when she went home the previous Friday evening, she reported to her father what had happened and how wonderful she now felt. His response was to spit upon a representative cross of Jesus Christ. His daughter was immediately demonically 'repossessed'.

Zakaria explained to the three women, that unless the victim became a real follower of Jesus, she would continue to be overwhelmed by Satan. The young woman instantly answered for herself. "I'm willing to become even a nun, but please relieve me from this repeated torment."

In Egypt, as in most countries in which Islam predominates, freedom of religion does not extend beyond freedom to choose Islam as one's religion.

Zakaria went further. He insisted that not only should the young woman confess Jesus as Lord, but that with the written consent of her mother and aunt, she should testify to a new beginning as a Christian by being baptised -immediately. Mother and aunt consented.

Placing a cross on the young woman's head, Zakaria commanded the demons to leave. They at first screamed their resistance, but finally were overwhelmed and ejected by the superior power available through Zakaria as a representative of Jesus.

Confession was made. The deed was sealed by baptism. The young woman who was now freed and full of the Spirit, returned home rejoicing. But this was not the end of the matter.

The following Saturday evening, an obviously affluent individual approached Zakaria at the conclusion of a church service. This was the Prosecutor General of the Provincial High Court of Gharbeyaa. Having introduced himself, he closely questioned Zakaria regarding the baptism of the young woman, without due regard to the legal requirements of the State.

In Egypt, as in most countries in which Islam predominates, freedom of religion does not extend beyond freedom to choose Islam as one's religion. Where a Muslim leaves that religion and chooses another, its classical law codes declare that one to be an apostate. As such, unless they can be persuaded or coerced to revert to the "one true faith", then that person's life may be forfeited. The legal sanction of death is to be administered by the state, or more frequently by immediate or close family members. In this way honour is claimed to be restored to the 'disgraced' family. For those who are responsible for the conversion, or baptism, the penalty may be imprisonment or worse.

Muslims converting to Christianity, mostly have a far more precise understanding of the implications of baptism, than their fellow Christians in the West. For them, following Jesus, literally means laying down their lives and dying to everything in the old life, just as Jesus (Luke 9:23) and Paul (Romans 6: 3-6) said it should.

The well-dressed stranger, having revealed his profession, then declared he was the young woman's uncle. He demanded confirmation and explanation of what Zakaria had done.

"I baptised her! What do you mean?" parried Zakaria.

"You put her in the water," the prosecutor asserted.

Zakaria, never one to be intimidated by confrontation or slow to grasp an opportunity, with apparent naive innocence replied, "Is that a crime? Are people prosecuted for bathing? What's your concern regarding this, unless of course you believe such events are of spiritual significance. If you are of the opinion that this event is unimportant, then let's leave it at that. On the other hand, if you are persuaded that this act evidences divine authority and power, then why deny yourself the privilege of enjoying and participating in the Almighty's provision?"

"Are you trying to baptise me as well?" fumed the prosecutor.

"Not really" replied Zakaria, "because as yet you still do not believe on Jesus."

Angrily the prosecutor threatened Zakaria with imprisonment.

To this Zakaria calmly replied, "Sir, do you know that it was in this very place that demons were expelled from your niece? And do you understand the significance of what transpired when after her first deliverance, her father spat on a cross? If you degrade Jesus and what he has done, then I can't be held responsible for the possibility that you too may become the habitation of demons. Imagine how it will look, when in the courtroom, you happen to be sitting in the judge's chair and right at that moment the demons force you to the floor and humiliate you before those present, as they used to do to your niece in front of her students in the classroom!"

Just the threat of this possibility was sufficient to prick the prosecutor's pride, pomposity and bluster. Deflated, he begged Zakaria for protection and well-being. He apologised and hastily departed, while at least a little of his reputation remained intact.

Having defended the faith from the possibilities of 'heresy' from a non-orthodox Christian group and from the personal intervention of the Provincial High Court Prosecutor, Zakaria strengthened the church's position even further. He wrote two books. One focused on the crucifixion of Christ. The other entitled *Salvation*, was about the necessity of redemption. Both were defence against an adversary far more dangerous than the 'Salvation of Souls' movement. This adversary had invaded Zakaria's land and had attempted to suppress his church for 14 centuries. This was Islam.

But the representatives of Islam would not organise to move against Zakaria just yet. They were not the only group who were starting to notice what was happening through Zakaria's revival ministry. There was another who would first call him to account - the Church.

Enter - The Church

Church history is replete with examples of God's Spirit attempting to break through in various new ways and unfortunately the church, through its appointees, resisting change or much which seemed new. The revival among some of the Coptic Orthodox congregations, appeared potentially to be more dangerous to the flock than alleged 'heresies' espoused by Protestants. Or so it seemed to some.

Complaints, motivated more perhaps by envy than desire for truth or maintenance of undisturbed orthodoxy, were sent to Coptic Pope Cyril VI, claiming Zakaria had become a Protestant! Within the community, a more serious charge could hardly be levelled. A clergy committee was expeditiously established to investigate the matter.

The board of inquiry consisted of two bishops, Gregorious and Shenouda, plus five priests. However on the day of the hearing in which Zakaria was to be cross-examined, Shenouda, later to become Pope Shenouda III, remained in his monastery at the request of Pope Cyril, because of unresolved conflict between the two of them.

Late 1967 was the time appointed to deal with the reportedly troublesome priest. To prepare, Zakaria fasted for three days and surrendered to whatever God planned for him.

A formal document was presented to Zakaria listing all the objections against him. This was duly signed by each complainant. But upon inspection, Zakaria noticed that all signatures were written by the same pen in the same handwriting. Even his own 'signature' was appended as one who opposed himself! The committee chose to disregard such minor oversights. It would be an understatement to suggest that the outcome of the committee's deliberations was a foregone conclusion, even before the accused had any opportunity to present his defence.

Zakaria was questioned regarding his concept of salvation. He defended himself, not so much from biblical text, which was not the final authority for the Orthodox community, but from the writings and sermons of the early Church Fathers. These were held in highest regard in matters relating to doctrine and practice.

Unable to demolish Zakaria's defence doctrinally, the committee turned its attention to matters of equal import. It was alleged that Zakaria had wept while preaching a sermon. Worse still, when the congregation was also moved to tears, Zakaria had done nothing to stop them. This was serious stuff indeed.

The interrogation report read, "This priest does not need to be questioned on theological or doctrinal issues; he simply deserves the severest church penalty to crush his pride. He should be removed from Tanta and returned to the small city of Shebeen where he was ordained, or to any other city the Pope sees fit."

In January 1968 Zakaria was duly prohibited from preaching and teaching and was formally suspended from all priestly functions for the duration of one year, presumably to atone for his sins and repent of the 'pride' which had moved him and his congregation to tears. To exacerbate the trauma of injustice, the family was ordered to depart the city before sunrise of the day following the suspension decision being handed down.

When Violet heard the news of Zakaria's suspension and their forced relocation, she was shocked and confused. She was also alarmed at the seeming injustice foisted upon them by the church. Her family had settled into their home and made new friends. The children were progressing well at school. Now they were to be uprooted and relocated without warning.

As Violet's prayers were mingled with her tears throughout the night, to the accompaniment of air force operations overhead and the wailing of friends below, the family hastily packed to leave. Of necessity they had to leave behind much of their furniture and clothing which invading rodents later destroyed. Zakaria encouraged them through this ordeal with words to which the Lord had drawn his attention:

> I will go before you and will level the mountains; I will break down gates of bronze and cut through bars of iron. I will give you the treasures of darkness, riches stored in secret places, so that you may know that I am the Lord... Who calls you by name (Isaiah 45: 2-3).

> A thousand may fall at your side, 10,000 at your right hand, but it will not come near you (Psalm 91:7).

CHAPTER 4

A BLESSED INTERLUDE

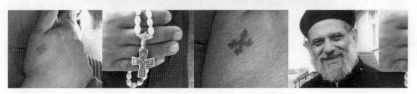

The family found shelter with relatives back in Damanhoor. The children were re-enrolled in a school in which their aunt was principal. Zakaria followed a daily routine. Four hours each day were spent travelling to and from Cairo where he attended a church service with the Pope. The rest of the day in Cairo was spent in the papal secretary's office. All of this time he spent in personal Bible study. At night at home he led Bible studies and prayer meetings till midnight.

Zakaria and Violet actually profited from the suspension. Freed from the frenetic pace of church life they were able to minister to their extended family of relatives. With reduced stress they were more relaxed to enjoy the peace and presence of God

Although Zakaria was prohibited from exercising any official priestly function, the work of the Holy Spirit through him could not be as easily closed down. Many who attended his nightly meetings chose to become followers of Jesus. Typical was Zakaria's younger brother, Maurice.

Toward the end of the scheduled meeting time, Maurice arrived to take Zakaria home. He waited downstairs for the meeting to conclude which, running to local time, it didn't. Finally, losing patience, Maurice angrily rushed upstairs to collect his would be passenger. The door to the meeting was open. Everyone was so engaged in prayer that they all failed to notice the arrival of the aggrieved Maurice, who was so smitten by the presence of God, that he surrendered his life to God and immediately, irrevocably quit his habit of smoking tobacco. Many others from these unofficial nocturnal gatherings went on to become founders and leaders of other ministries in the Damanhoor region and beyond.

On January 6 1969, Pope Cyril on short notice asked Zakaria to conduct the Christmas service in a new church in Maniel El Radaa. It had recently been constructed in the fundamentalist Islamist area controlled by Jamaat El Islamia. The Egyptian Constitution prohibits building any church within 200 metres of an established mosque. This provision makes it extremely difficult ever to build a Christian church anywhere, assuming one could get government approval. Whenever plans for such construction may be approved, a minor miracle in itself, Muslims not infrequently move to establish a mosque in the assigned area, thus precluding the possibility of any comparable Christian construction. For reasons unknown, no such action was initiated on this occasion.

Because of the history of the area, Christians were unsurprisingly afraid to attend meetings in their new building. Nevertheless, Zakaria managed to conduct the new church's first Christmas service without incident.

Obviously Zakaria did nothing to offend, because in February 1969, Pope Cyril issued instructions for Zakaria to be appointed to St Marks in New Cairo. From being a young and inexperienced priest in the small town of Shebeen, Zakaria was now to resume his official priestly duties and ministry, prominently placed within the precincts of the nation's capital city.

"For (what) the Lord Almighty has purposed... Who can thwart him? His hand is stretched out and who can turn it back (Isaiah 14:27)".

Quite so. How true.

CHAPTER 5

CAIRO CROWDS

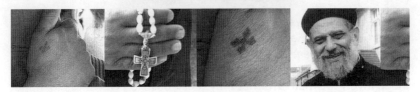

Miles of Miracles

In March 1969, Zakaria commenced ministry at St Marks in Cairo. The church was located in Cleopatra Street. As the street name suggests, this was an affluent, prestigious suburb. The church was designed and painted in the finest Italian traditions. It still is one of the most outstanding examples of its genre in Cairo. Pope Cyril was obviously sympathetic toward his priest to have given him such an appointment, while at the same time encouraging him to "preach his heart out".

In addition to the main sanctuary, an adjacent three-storey building could simultaneously accommodate an overflow of thousands of worshippers.

When Zakaria commenced his weekly meetings, just 15 people were in attendance. But as congregants invited friends to meet with and hear their new priest, numbers increased. During 1970 as a result of miraculous healings and exorcisms, attendance grew even more rapidly. Beyond personal testimony and word-of-mouth, meetings were not advertised. In such a charged environment, people were inevitably drawn to seek God through prayer, always hoping their own ailments and weaknesses might be the next to attract divine favour.

As healings and deliverances multiplied, so too did the witness of those who had been touched by God. Friends brought friends who brought friends. Curiosity also drew onlookers literally by the truckload. In addition to physical needs being met in abundance, spiritual needs were also attended to. Many discovered Jesus for the first time in their lives.

Zakaria's practice was to beseech God to heal the sick, if in each case it was God's will. He simultaneously encouraged the exercise of faith by the afflicted person, if that was possible, as well as in those who had accompanied that person to the meetings. He always asked for those involved whether or not they really believed Christ could in fact still heal today. Only when the answer was in the affirmative did he proceed. Tuesday evening meetings became known as the miracle night.

Frequently meetings descended into chaos through demonic manifestations in the lives of those who attended. Screams and yelling rent the air, shattering the peace, till Zakaria commanded the demons in the name of Jesus, that they remain silent.

They instantly obeyed the Lord and his servant. At the conclusion of each meeting, those oppressed by demonic influence proceeded to the front of the main auditorium, whereupon they were often thrown to the ground and caused to scream in rage, until Zakaria dealt deliverance to each of the afflicted.

Many would be taken backstage to be ministered to, while a gathered group sang and prayed. As Zakaria prayed over individuals, each was freed. Many were healed from physical ailments following their exorcism. In this manner a young lady who had been blind, received her sight. A young man who had been stabbed in the throat with a knife was instantly healed.

One evening a group of medical doctors arrived. They had heard about what was happening and were both concerned and somewhat sceptical. They thought that the thrashing around on the floor of some people, was the result of involuntary epilepsy attacks. They carefully examined people who had responded to and for ministry. Their conclusion was that the only explanation possible was that this was the work of God. To demonstrate their wholehearted support, they presented Zakaria with a gift of $3,000 to purchase chairs for the auditorium. This amount of money was the equivalent of 8 years of average income!

Tawfik El Hakeem was one of Egypt's best-known writers. He was an outstanding philosopher. He was also a Muslim. Some of his friends asked Zakaria if he would pray for El Hakeem's wife who was paralysed. Zakaria agreed. The following week when the woman was brought, Zakaria asked his usual question, whether or not she believed

As healings and deliverances multiplied, so too did the witness of those who had been touched by God.

Jesus could heal her. When she answered in the affirmative Zakaria prayed. Her feet, legs and arms immediately regained feeling and strength. She was healed. Her husband could not help but notice what had happened to his wife. The next week he came to the meeting.

New Revelations

El Hakeem was easily recognisable by the coat and hat he usually wore in which he was often photographed by the media. He listened attentively to that night's message and joined in some of the singing. He also remained to observe the healing session. When the evening's activities were all complete, he was able to speak with Zakaria personally. They began meeting weekly in El Hakeem's home on Wednesday afternoons. El Hakeem was the first person to point out to Zakaria inconsistencies and internal contradictions within Islam.

On their very first meeting alone, they spent three hours discussing Islam. When Zakaria left, he drove only as far as the top of the street, parked his car and wrote down everything he could remember from their conversation. It had been quite a revelation. Until that time Zakaria had been engrossed in defending Christianity against (false) claims made against it by Islam. Now for the first time, his attention was drawn to examine more closely the various unsustainable positions and claims of Islam itself.

The penetrating observations of El Hakeem, a Muslim scholar himself, led Zakaria to conclude that part of his future ministry and mission should be in bringing these matters to light, for the benefit of those who followed their unexamined faith - Muslims themselves. This was a critical turning point in Zakaria's understanding of his future. It was also fraught with danger, for Islam historically admitted critical evaluation of neither its beliefs nor its practices.

The life and sayings of its proclaimed prophet, Mohammad, were considered of divine origin. Over the centuries, these were carefully collected, edited and codified in what today is known as the Quran and the Traditions. Within these volumes are what seem to be many contradictions, at least to infidels – ie non-Muslims. But to the faithful, these are not matters open to question or even reinterpretation. To do so could invite defying death.

'Revelations' alleged to be of divine origin via the angel Gabriel, formed the holy book, the Quran. Those same revelations certified Mohammad's prophethood and enthroned Allah as the supreme and only divine being. Mohammad authenticated the Quran, which in turn authenticated Mohammad. This closed circle of mutual authentication was buttressed by 14 centuries of implacable opposition to anything and anyone who dared to contest its claims.

Any who tried would be dealt with swiftly and severely. But what if the whole edifice was only a facade of deception, held together by compulsion and coercion rather than self-evident, coherent, defensible truth? Tantalising questions indeed!

From 15 to 5,000

The meetings at St Mark's grew from 15 up to 5,000 people. Each floor of the complex was crowded. Closed-circuit television, a first for

Egypt, was installed. People who attended meetings would frequently call friends and family to tell them to watch Father Zakaria on national television.

For 10 years Zakaria taught from the Song of Solomon in the Old Testament and from the book of Revelation, in the New Testament, much to the delight, fascination and edification of his hearers. Christians were intrigued by Revelation's end times images and Muslims were attracted to the sensual nature of Solomon's writings. Zakaria also preached the good news about Jesus. Throughout it all, the Spirit of God was powerfully present doing what only he could do, healing, releasing and drawing people to a vital faith in and experience of Jesus Christ.

Zakaria continued faithfully discharging his priestly responsibilities and conducting weekly church services, along with other duties of his office. But increasingly he had to spend time reading, researching and studying to prepare himself to teach and minister at the weekly 'miracle' services. To allow for this, each Tuesday and Thursday he would withdraw to the Mokatam Mountains, about one hour's drive beyond the bustle and pollution of Cairo. There he would seek God alone for the message and the anointing, through which lives were being radically transformed.

Back in the large church complex, from 3.30 p.m. on afternoons when evening meetings were being held, television-linked rooms would start to fill with expectant people. For three hours they would sing and worship, inviting the Lord to presence himself in their midst.

Shortly after 7.00 p.m. Zakaria would arrive. He commenced each meeting by answering questions from the congregation, after which he would preach.

His sermons were usually based upon verse by verse teaching through consecutive passages of Scripture. Each passage was divided into three alliterate or rhyming headings to aid memorisation. Applications to daily life abounded. Sometimes he was a fiery evangelist. At other times he was a gentle pastor, encouraging his people to walk closely with the Great Shepherd of the sheep. He was also frequently breaking open the Word to reveal hidden meanings, to strengthen and spiritually nourish his people. Those styles might vary, but the underlying message was always the same, to confess and repent of sin, to accept Jesus and to allow him to change wayward lives instantly.

He preached passionately. The Spirit and non-Christian outsiders showed up and lives were changed never to be the same again. New believers were assigned to cell groups, which were spontaneously springing up throughout New Cairo.

These met daily for prayer, Bible study, worship and meditation. Government office employees worked only until 2.00p.m. and were thereafter free to participate each afternoon in church cell life, while attending evening meetings to seek after God as time permitted.

Willing Workers

Egyptian summer holidays last for four months. Therefore new believers among university students and others had ample time available to be involved in ministry. Much of this was directed toward the disadvantaged or extremely poor people in the city.

Other teams focused on going further afield to unreached villages with the good news. There were daily and weekly outreach tours which travelled in hired buses. Each day hundreds of homes were visited. Every Friday 10 minibuses, each holding 15 eager evangelists, headed out to Upper and Lower Egypt. Even the bus drivers joined in preaching to whomever they met.

A wide variety of isolated, uneducated and completely unchurched Christians were contacted. Not knowing the significance of various practices, they had simply followed the customs of Muslim neighbours while still considering themselves Christians. Some had named their sons Mohammad. Others were fasting during the Islamic holy month of Ramadan. Still others were in the habit of availing themselves of the services of Muslim Sheiks to read the Quran and pray on the occasion of family funerals. They were totally oblivious to the weightier dangers of creating a hybrid religion or heresy.

Some of the workers dedicated themselves to visiting the sick and lonely in hospitals. Others scanned the death notices in local newspapers, to attend funerals in support of grieving families and friends. They also took the opportunity to witness to them about the eternal hope beyond death, found only through believing in and depending exclusively on the resurrected Jesus.

At the conclusion of a hospital visit to one congregational member, at the request of a nearby patient, one team prayed for a Muslim man who had been paralysed for two years as a result of an horrific accident.

Having prayed for him, the believers shared some Scripture with him and also left him with a copy of the Gospel of Matthew. When they returned the next day, the man advised the team he had finished reading the gospel and asked for more. At this point the visitation team requested Zakaria himself to visit the hospital to pray for the new acquaintance, Mohammad.

Upon arrival at the bedside, having placed the cross which he always wore with his other priestly garments, on the paralysed person's head, Zakaria, full of faith, prayed for Mohammad's complete healing. Because the man's feet actually moved, he decided to attend a meeting of the church, in his wheelchair.

Thereafter two of the church leaders collected Mohammad each week to deliver him to the church, whereupon he was carried up to the second floor of the auditorium and placed in the front row. There he heard the message about Jesus and decided to trust him for his eternal security. In many Middle Eastern and Asian countries, one's name is the primary indication of to which religious community one belongs. The name Mohammad obviously signified the person was a Muslim. In that he now wanted to become a follower of Jesus, the paralysed person decided he needed a new name. Not surprisingly, he chose the name 'Zakaria'.

After his baptism, God spoke to the newly named 'Zakaria' through a vision. He was foretold that his namesake, Fr Zakaria, at a future meeting would command him to get up from his wheelchair, after which he would walk 12 steps. When Fr Zakaria heard of the vision, he called for believers to meet in a home, to pray fervently for the next stage of the new 'Zakaria's' healing. As was revealed, exactly that happened. On Fr Zakaria's command, 'Zakaria' stood up, walked 12 steps, and then sat down again in his wheelchair.

For a second time, Jesus appeared to 'Zakaria' in a vision, to advise him that Fr Zakaria would pray for him once more. When that happened, he would get up, walk and keep walking. He would have no further need of his wheelchair.

It was during a Tuesday night meeting when 'Zakaria' was brought up onto the platform. There, as the crowd watched expectantly, Fr Zakaria prayed for him. Fr Zakaria next commanded him, in the name of Jesus, to stand, walk and keep walking.

To the thunderous applause of the excited worshippers, it all unfolded once more, exactly as had been foretold in the second vision. For the next few weeks his now vacated wheelchair remained on the platform, as a solemn reminder of the presence and power of the living Lord - Jesus.

News of what had happened spread rapidly through the narrow alleys and streets of crowded Cairo. Jesus had generated as much news there, as he had in Jerusalem almost two millennia previously.

With the expansion of the ministry, it was obvious more leaders were needed than could be provided through ordained clergy. Zakaria designed a comprehensive curriculum, covering the basics of doctrinal belief and the practice of ministry. Twenty people were recruited and trained on site. Single men lived in the ministry premises in Menies Street, New Cairo. Married men travelled in each day

This was a novel innovation to attempt to cope with the exigencies of the situation. Historically, only ordained clergy were deployed within the Coptic Church. But an unprecedented visitation by God, called forth an unprecedented response. Zakaria's new team or 'association', of full-time lay workers, was called the 'Ministry of the Generation to Come.'

On the three floors of the ministry premises, daily work continued unabated. Two additional villas in a nearby suburb were obtained to accommodate orphaned children and elderly folk in need of care. At the time, these premises were valued at in excess of 2 million Egyptian pounds. They had been bought and donated to the work, by a very rich family whom Zakaria had personally led to the Lord. Mistakenly the Pope assumed they had become Zakaria's personal property.

The Menies Street facilities were used as headquarters for administration. From here, one team led by Sergeant Fawzy of the Egyptian army, with military precision, weekly prepared and posted 1200 outreach packets. These materials were sent to Cairenes whose names and addresses were extracted from the local telephone directory.

A second team worked at printing and publishing Christian literature designed to equip and encourage believers. Other literature was specially prepared for outreach purposes. To accelerate the process, one of the earliest computers taken into Egypt, was imported. It was so large it took up half the size of a normal room. It could also operate only in controlled conditions in temperatures constantly kept lower than that which is normal for Cairo. For this purpose, two large air-conditioners were imported and installed.

A third team was responsible for tape recording all of Zakaria's messages. These were then copied and posted to people throughout the country. Those who attended the meetings were able to purchase their own copies as they left the auditorium.

Some members of these teams were actually people who had converted from Islam. A dentist was one such. Three decades later he still remembered and recounted with affectionate warmth, the excitement of those early days.

Children's Capers

Zakaria was under constant pressure from people and the various tasks for which he was officially responsible. But even when others were prevented from interrupting him, his son Peter was always an exception. Whenever Peter barged into his office, he always stopped whatever he was involved in, to welcome Peter's spontaneous embraces and respond in kind to his kisses.

Peter's older sister Janet, compared with her brothers, was a most obedient child who would do anything to avoid upsetting her parents. When Zakaria travelled overseas he brought back modest presents for the children. For Janet he bought appropriate girl outfits. When the congregation saw her wearing her new clothes they complained. To restore peace she was obliged to give up wearing what her father had bought for her. Her brothers were perhaps more deserving of censure.

Beshay was a kindly but vigilantly observant Christian cobbler, who lived on the ground floor of the Zakaria family's apartment block. Any misbehaviour by the children was duly noted and reported by him to Zakaria, as he nightly returned home. Zakaria was very affectionate towards his children. It just didn't seem so to the boys, especially when appropriate punishment was administered by him to the seat of their pants. It didn't take long for the boys to uncover their nemesis, who regularly would despoil their childhood pranks. Their counteroffensive was pin-equipped paper darts targeting Beshay's bald pate at a distance of twenty paces, from the third floor above.

Zakaria attempted to be a loving and tender parent, but like many others in ministry, his priority was service to the Lord and his church rather than to his family. Nevertheless, in spite of the heavy demands upon him, he made time for an annual visit by the family back to see relatives in Damanhoor. He also personally tutored the children in year 12 Arabic.

Zakaria was required to travel extensively throughout Egypt as an instrument of the spreading revival. Conversions were multiplying. Believers were being strengthened and built up. New workers were being recruited and trained continuously, to support the divine fire spreading throughout the land.

Priestly Promotion

Fr Macary Younan was one worker who rose to prominence. Prior to his ordination to the priesthood, he was known as Sabry. His wife had attended Zakaria's weekly Tuesday and Thursday evening meetings. Eventually, she made a personal commitment to become a follower of

Jesus. Thereafter she diligently prayed for her husband's conversion. One night Zakaria visited the couple in their home. After some discussion, Sabry agreed to surrender his life to Jesus. Together they prayed. The spiritual transaction was completed. Sabry never looked back.

It took little time to recognise that he had an amazing voice for singing. He was also a very gifted, creative composer of lyrics and music. While Zakaria preached, Sabry listened, composed lyrics and music to match the theme of the nightly message and at the end stepped up to sing the gospel.

Zakaria was required to travel extensively throughout Egypt as an instrument of the spreading revival. Conversions were multiplying.

After years of working together, Zakaria nominated Sabry to be considered for ordination as a priest in the Coptic Orthodox Church. Assuit, a city in Upper Egypt, was chosen for the ordination service. A local bishop presided. In the packed church the temperature soared to over 40°C.

For whatever reason, prior to the commencement of the service, the local bishop gave Zakaria permission to preach however he chose, but there were local conventions which should not be breached. One was a prohibition against using a handkerchief to mop one's brow while preaching. The other was that the heavy outer garment normally worn by all priests, could not be removed under any circumstances.

As Zakaria preached, inside his garment was becoming more like a sauna. Perspiration poured from him and was absorbed into his robes. They in turn became heavier and heavier. Totally focused on his own message, when it climaxed with Elijah throwing aside his garment, Zakaria did exactly that without thinking.

As the priestly garment sailed out into the crowd, one can only imagine what the local bishop may have been thinking. In more ways than one, Zakaria was an iconoclast, always stripping away that which was unnecessary, to reveal the heart of the matter.

Another of Zakaria's assistants was a fellow, who upon ordination, became known as Fr Samaan Ibrahim from the Mokatem region. He was a very spiritual, hard-working, self-sacrificing man of God. He responded to the Lord's call to establish a ministry in the village of El Zarayeb. As the name in Arabic implies, this was a community of garbage collectors. Their lives and habitation were extremely impoverished. Through Fr Samaan's diligence and compassion for these the poorest of the poor, the ministry grew. Today there can be up to 10,000 people in attendance at his worship services. A prayer conference the church held in May 2005 drew some 20,000 believers.

Outwitting the Law

In 1972 Muslim extremists attacked and burnt a church in El Khanka. Zakaria hastened to the scene, took photographs, collected burnt bricks, books and other items as conclusive evidence of what had transpired. The next day he met with a group of fellow priests in Cairo, to show them the evidence and decide what response to make. They decided to hold a demonstration, a church service and prayer meeting on the same site the next day. Some less courageous clergy, privy to the decision, reported the plan to government officials and private investigators.

To avoid further inflammation of a volatile situation, armed police ringed the suburb to prevent outsiders entering. But Zakaria had arrived before the blockade was in place. Following a worship service, Zakaria gathered together local believers, to encourage them further. Having achieved his purposes for coming, Zakaria was confronted with the reverse of the dilemma of the earlier challenge. Having got in, he now had to get out.

Police roadblocks delineated by orange coloured markers, straddled every exit. Officers were determined to question passengers of every car leaving the area. Zakaria was a very high-profile person, because of the spreading reputation and effectiveness of his ministry in Cairo.

Police interrogations in Egypt, as in many other countries of the region, are not restricted by the niceties of legal convention. Zakaria had good reason to fear for his own safety and for that of those travelling with him, if they were stopped, questioned and recognised. Ever the entrepreneur, rising to the challenge of the situation, Zakaria had a motorcyclist precede their car to kick aside the plastic barricades as he wove through them. Zakaria and his party were able to speed straight through, before the police realised what was happening.

Not every incident concluded so swiftly or happily. The Christian life is frequently more battleground than playground. Ultimate victory is assured, but on occasion its attainment might seem inordinately delayed. This would be so for Zakaria. The presenting problems which would silence Zakaria's powerful, popular, public ministry arose from a jealous bishop and an infamous article.

Troubling Times

In the mid-1970s, Zakaria visited a Coptic monastery and heard a sermon on the love and grace of Jesus. He was so impressed by the monk's presentation, he mentioned him to the recently elected Pope Shenouda. In the Coptic Orthodox Church, only priests may marry. Monks must remain celibate and only the celibate can become bishops or Popes. The Pope requested Zakaria to encourage the monk to accept an appointment to become a bishop at which task he was successful.

Following the monk's ordination, Zakaria invited the new bishop to preach at St Mark's. This was so well received by the congregation that agreement was reached for him to preach regularly on the first Tuesday of each month. But after the third month, the bishop ceased preaching on the love of God and pursued instead more intellectual, philosophical subjects. The congregation reacted. Interest declined. Within a comparatively brief time, attendance declined from 3,000 to a mere handful. The bishop was mystified. He concluded that the difference in numbers between his and Zakaria's congregations, was that the latter must be attracting larger numbers by teaching non-orthodox or Protestant doctrines, since the Protestants were the only other group to attract large numbers of people. Having listened unsuccessfully to hundreds of Zakaria's sermons to find evidence to support his hypothesis, he nevertheless lodged a formal complaint with Pope Shenouda.

The more substantial issue which was used to silence Zakaria was an article which appeared in the church magazine. Zakaria had not written it, but as editor-in-chief he was responsible for everything in the magazine. A member of St Mark's ministry team had written a poetic reflection on the crucifixion of Christ. In the poem, the writer said that if one could have been an eyewitness to the crucifixion, the wounding of Jesus would have so moved him, as to have been 'justified at that moment'. By his use of that phrase, he was trying to convey the possibility of one's being declared guiltless before God because of Christ's death on the cross for all, which makes possible a person's coming into a right relationship with God the moment one believes on Jesus. While poetic license might admit some latitude, orthodox theology did not, especially if on the hunt for a possible heretic.

A fierce attack was hatched indirectly aimed at Zakaria. The Coptic Church's official magazine, El Karaza published a series of articles entitled, *The Heresy of Salvation in a Moment.* Zakaria concluded that he was the real target. To prepare for the defence which would be inevitably required of him, he surveyed all the writings pertaining to the subject, written and published in El Karaza by Pope Shenouda himself. In one of his articles, the Pope had written "Blessed is this moment when Augustine was converted from sinner to saint, not from sinner to repentant soul but from sinner to saint."

The clear inference was that salvation occurs in a moment of time as a person believes on Jesus. Hence, the Pope, by speaking of Augustine's conversion, appeared to agree with Zakaria's understanding of the doctrine and processes of salvation. None of this lessened the believer's responsibility to live a godly life as much as possible. News of the controversy was reported beyond Egypt. The April 7 1978 edition of Christianity Today carried a comprehensive article on views contested within the Coptic Church.

On April 17 1978 in a publicly delivered sermon, Zakaria quoted many of the Pope's own sayings on the subject in support of his own position. Quotations attributed to the Pope were subsequently regarded as not material to the case and were overlooked, but Zakaria's sermon was not. Following the April 17 sermon, the Pope requested Zakaria in writing, to cease his public ministry forthwith and to await the outcome of an official trial conducted by the church. The charge would be heresy.

It would be 9 years before a date was set for the trial. At the hearing before a bishop and three priests, the bishop dictated both questions and answers to a scribe. Zakaria was not asked even a single question. Like salvation, the trial would be completed 'in a moment of time'.

CHAPTER 6

SOME LABOURS LOST

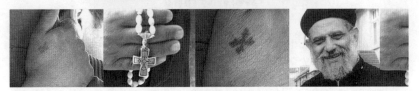

Zakaria was no longer permitted the privilege of public ministry. He was barred from conducting worship or preaching. After 10 amazing years in which the Holy Spirit had been so obviously validating Zakaria's ministry, the weekly Tuesday and Thursday evening meetings were closed. Thousands of disappointed attendees were outraged. They vented their frustration, deluging church officials with letters and petitions supporting Zakaria's reinstatement. It was all to no avail.

The decision to suspend Zakaria from ministry devastated his 3 older children, Janet, Feyez and Ben. They were so hurt that they decided not to attend church any more. Violet had to use her parental authority to coerce their attendance. She herself was so adversely emotionally affected that she was unable to sit in church without weeping because her husband was no longer permitted to officiate

But the suspension did have one good side effect. Family life improved greatly because Zakaria was more available. The youngest son Peter was a prime beneficiary. He was able to access his father's attention and skills in ways which had formerly been denied his older siblings at that earlier stage in their lives. Zakaria helped Peter with his study of English, talked and joked with him and started to become more than a religious "father" to his own children.

The children noticed that even his style of discipline changed. In the event of discipline needing to be enforced or punishment for its infringement needing to be meted out Zakaria would first explain the nature of the wrongdoing. Then he would instruct about his responsibility under God to administer correction, followed by spanking with a ruler. The episode concluded with hugs, kisses and the restoration of love and trust.

Redirected Efforts

But Zakaria was hardly idle. He could be occupied with his 'association' in Menies. Weekly private meetings could still be conducted on the premises. 300 leaders had been trained and were happy to work under Zakaria's leadership. House meetings, village and hospital outreach, continued as before. People still continued to come to various meetings, but not in the same numbers. As often happens in the church, when the shepherd is struck, the sheep scatter. New believers especially became confused by all the rumours and counter rumours. They opted out. However for the willing, there was always a way forward.

If Zakaria could no longer officiate as a priest, he would find other ways in which to cause growth in God's kingdom. Up to this time he had prioritised evangelism. Now he would turn his attention to discipleship. Toward that end he designed a curriculum spread over eight books for use within small groups.

The first of these, *Receiving Christ,* focused on becoming a Christian by accepting what Jesus had achieved in God's redemptive plan of salvation and by personally coming to him in faith. The second, *Standing Firm,* helped new believers to understand the fatherhood of God, his care and provision for his children. In this Zakaria stressed the importance of personal daily devotional times, Scripture memorisation, witnessing and other basics of the Christian life.

The third level of teaching aimed to assist believers to grow in the Lord. The first part, *Growth A,* encouraged people to meditate on the life and character of Jesus. The second part, *Growth B,* aimed to guide believers into full surrender to the Lordship of Jesus. The final stage was that of spiritual maturity, in which believers were encouraged to allow the Holy Spirit to direct every aspect of their lives. At the conclusion of the Bible study series, believers were invited to choose a preferred area of ministry for further training. This could be small group leadership, training of other leaders or evangelism.

Each of the books was approximately 250 pages. Every page was handwritten by Zakaria, photocopied and collated by others. By this means, hundreds of people were nurtured in discipleship and trained to become leaders. This curriculum is still followed by many congregations in various countries today. The 9 years of being forced to abandon public ministry were not completely lost.

In 1980, Zakaria decided to renovate and expand the Menies premises. Although building permits were not legally required, local officials still denied permission for the work. Unbeknown to Zakaria, this denial was but the first skirmish in a long battle orchestrated by government against him. President Anwar El Sadat sent one of his officials to inform Zakaria that he was very impressed with Zakaria's work. Allegedly because of this, the President himself was pleased to accede to the request to renovate and expand the church.

Zakaria was curious to know how the President even knew of his existence, let alone his work. Through inquiry, he learned that President Sadat was in conflict with Pope Shenouda and had hoped to use Zakaria to retaliate against the Pope. All that was required on Zakaria's part, was a letter confirming his acceptance of the President's offer.

Fortunately, the Lord himself for some time had been impressing upon Zakaria, the need to submit completely to those in authority. Even though the authorities in the church were seemingly treating him so unjustly, his allegiance to the church had to precede that to the State. He had taught others about submission to God and his anointed agents, now it was his turn to heed his own teaching.

After a night of prayer, instead of accepting the almost unheard of opportunity afforded to him by the President, he wrote to President Sadat thanking him for his kind proposal, but declining the offer because the matter needed to be first approved by Pope Shenouda III. Concurrently he wrote to the Pope, advising him he was ceasing the ministry of his lay association and would present the ministry's premises for use at the discretion of the Pope himself. The Pope had mistakenly formed the view that Zakaria had been using his popularity more for money than ministry. Accumulation of personal wealth was not unknown among Coptic clergy, but Zakaria had never given way to that temptation.

One might have thought that following such willing and generous submission and an unquestioned demonstration of integrity on Zakaria's part, the matter of the largely false charge against him, would have been expeditiously dealt with and he would have been honourably reinstated to full priestly privileges and responsibilities. Not so. It would take a further six years to finalise the charge in the church against him. There would also be the additional test of 318 days in prison as a guest of the government!

CHAPTER 7

IMPRISONED

A Night to Remember

On Wednesday September 2, 1981 at 10:30 p.m., Zakaria returned home from visiting his people and soon retired for a well earned rest. But at 1:30 a.m. he was woken by his son Ben, telling him someone was banging on their apartment door. At first, because of the unusual lateness of the hour, Zakaria tried to ignore the insistent knocking, hoping the caller would go away. That didn't happen. Eventually as the noise increased, Zakaria went to the door to see who it could be. Unfortunately whoever it was on the outside, had covered the peep hole deliberately to prevent Zakaria being able to see them. Zakaria threatened to summon the police immediately if they did not desist and depart forthwith. The answer was, "We are the police!"

Mindful of recent incidents in which Christians had been murdered by zealous Muslims belonging to a well-known local group, Jamaat El Islamia, Zakaria asked for proof of identity. The covering over the peep hole was removed to reveal a uniformed police officer holding his badge of office for Zakaria to see, while another threatened to smash the door down unless Zakaria opened it immediately.

As the intensity of the conflict escalated, not surprisingly, other sleepy neighbours disturbed by the commotion, turned on their lights, opened their doors and came out to see what the racket was all about. Eventually, Zakaria had no option other than to open the door to confront his nocturnal inquisitors. Immediately ten soldiers, sundry uniformed police non-commissioned officers and plainclothes members of the secret police, surged into the apartment.

Brandishing a court-ordered arrest warrant, they hustled Zakaria back into that part of the cramped living room which doubled as his 'study' and ordered him to sit. While two soldiers held pistols to Zakaria's head, others commenced a systematic search of the entire premises. When that was completed, Zakaria was removed to a police station. His son Feyez was dragooned into using the family's vehicle to transport three of the soldiers to their destination.

Zakaria was left alone until 3:30 a.m., when he was shocked to be joined by Bishoy Yassa, a parish priest of St George's Coptic Church in Heliopolis. He was well-known for his gentle, humble and loving demeanour. His was a life of prayer.

At 4.00a.m. the two priests were escorted to police cars already filled with soldiers. In response to Fr Bishoy's inquiry as to their destination, the reply was, 'El Marg', a dreaded place of internment, well-known to all Cairenes. Upon arrival, after a 30 minute journey of ordered silence, the priests were body searched and with their few permitted possessions, were swallowed into the innermost bowels of the prison. It was now 5.00a.m. and their new address was cell 18. Typically it was small and very dark.

On the inside of the cell door Zakaria could just make out an inscription scratched by an inmate who had been relocated perhaps mere moments before the new prisoners' arrival. It read, 'The black days are over... 5.6.81 - 3.9.81'. Zakaria couldn't imagine how someone could have survived in this darkened dungeon-like existence for a whole three months! Somewhat disturbed by such a prospect, he later asked prison authorities to paint over the reminder of another's grief and suffering. Like so many others of their profession, the guards promised much but delivered little.

Initially the two priests assumed that they had been incarcerated lest they cause trouble, prior to an important presidential speech in two days time on September 5. Then more Christians started to arrive; bishops, priests and lay leaders. They were all placed three to a cell, each cell measuring 1.8 x 1.5 x 1.8 metres. At first Fr Athanasius was put into Zakaria's cell, but he was replaced by Frs. Samuel and Tadros Malaty respectively. Eventually this section of El Marg's 28 prison cells was completely filled with Christian leaders, all rounded up to enjoy the dubious privilege of being 'guests' of the Egyptian government until someone, somewhere decided otherwise.

The three prisoners in each cell shared two mattresses. For personal convenience, a hole in the floor was designated officially as 'the toilet'.

> **None of course knew exactly why they had been arrested. Christians ... were viewed as second-class citizens or "dhimmis" by the authorities and Muslim population.**

Samir, an inmate in an adjacent cell, who because of his political activities had previously experienced prison life, was able to advise the bewildered newcomers of prison rules and regulations. Listed among these was the right of prisoners to speak with one another.

Upon learning this, each introduced himself to all others. The subsequent tally revealed that the recent arrivals included no fewer than 8 bishops, 24 priests and a significant number of Christian lay leaders. This surely represented one of the most important involuntary ecclesiastical gatherings in recent Egyptian church history.

None of course knew exactly why they had been arrested. Overlooking such legal niceties was hardly unprecedented in Egyptian practice, especially when applied to Christians who were viewed as second-class citizens or "dhimmis" by the authorities and Muslim population.

Those among them, who had a degree of political sophistication, were of the opinion that they had been innocently caught up in national issues. President Anwar El Sadat was preparing to break ranks with the longstanding Arab position regarding recognition of Israel as an independent state. Since the United Nations' recognition of Israel over three decades previously, no Muslim government in the world had been prepared to accept its existence. Most were and remain committed to its elimination, for Islamic theological reasons. Sadat had to take every precaution to maintain Egyptian unity and that included the possibility of suppressing religiously based sedition.

Therefore, he determined to arrest all political opponents with the potential to mobilise crowds and public opinion against establishing a fragile Middle East peace through recognition of Israel. Opposition to his regime and policies would not be tolerated, irrespective of from which religious community it emanated. In the government's pre-emptive strike Christians and Muslims, at least in this respect, would be treated equally.

Even Coptic Pope Shenouda was restrained by government and exiled to his monastery for a few years. None of course, ever knew the real reasons behind the government's sudden oppression. Single party ruling authorities are not subject to the vagaries of the ballot box. Their power is derived from the party not the people. This power through the party is to be retained at all costs. Suppression of dissent is one of the more common means employed by such governments.

One truth the prisoners knew for certain. It was a very hot 45° in their unventilated cells. To try to access the slightest breath of fresh air which might sneak in beneath the steel door of their enclosure, Zakaria lay down on the bare cement floor. Eventually he contracted a kidney infection.

As his pain intensified during the night, his fellow priests banged on their cell doors. The warden on duty successfully sought permission to relieve Zakaria's pain temporarily, by means of an intravenous injection. Unfortunately for the patient, the temporary relief was almost worse than the ailment. The male nurse, Am Nobi, was hardly a ministering angel. As a chronic diabetic, his vision was significantly impaired.

When, because of Am Nobi's poor eyesight, the needle of the syringe missed Zakaria's vein, rather than removing it to try again, the nurse left it under the skin, manoeuvring it around in a futile attempt to locate the uncooperative vein. For 30 minutes Am Nobi the night nurse, gouged and probed without success, much to Zakaria's physical discomfort.

Chapter 1: Out from obscurity - **Feyez, a youth leader, enjoyed playing the guitar with the youth and church leaders at St George's Church in Damanhoor Egypt (1954).**

Chapter 2: The Call - **Feyez and Violet's wedding ceremony at St George's Church in Damanhoor Egypt (February, 1st 1959).**

Chapter 2: The Call - **Ordination ceremony at the Coptic Church in Shebeen El Kom Egypt (February, 8th 1959).**

Chapter 3: God Steps In - **The Botross' family in Tanta: Fr Zakaria, Violet, Janet, Feyez & Benjamin (1966).**

Chapter 3: God Steps In - **Fr Zakaria prays over Baptismal water in preparation for the very first baptism of a Muslim convert (Yousef) in Tanta, Egypt (1964).**

Chapter 5: Cairo Crowds - **Fr Zakaria with members of the congregation of St Mark's Church in Cleopatra Egypt during a day retreat to the Pyramids (1970).**

Chapter 5: Cairo Crowds - **Fr Zakaria preaches on the third floor of St Mark's church hall in Cleopatra, New Cairo, Egypt. Thousands of people packed the three story building every Tuesday and Thursday night to hear and watch Fr Zakaria through closed circuit TV.**

Chapter 10: People, Police and Prisons - **Fr Zakaria together with Fr Girguis Sophi in a spiritual retreat for the youth leaders of St. George's Church Heliopolis Egypt in 1988.**

Chapter 11: Exiled In Australia - **On the night of his arrival to Melbourne, Australia, Fr Zakaria meets with Bishop Isaiah and the Coptic priests at St Mary's Church Kensington (November 5th, 1989).**

Chapter 11: Exiled In Australia - **Fr Zakaria and Violet meets with His Holiness Pope Shenouda III (Coptic Pope) during his first visit to Melbourne, Australia (1989).**

Chapter 11: Exiled In Australia - **The first gathering of His Holiness Pope Shenouda the third wit Coptic priests in Sydney, Australia (1989).**

Chapter 11: Exiled In Australia - **Fr Zakaria with members of the congregation of St. George's Church, Melbourne, Australia, at a family retreat (1991).**

Chapter 12; Sudan In England - **Shortly after his arrival to England Fr Zakaria meets with members of the congregation of St Mary's Church in Brighton (1993).**

Chapter 12; Sudan In England - **Fr Zakaria celebrates His Holiness Pope Shenouda's visit to dedicate the iconostasis at St Mary's Church in Brighton England (2000).**

Chapter 12; Sudan In England - **Celebrating the baptism of a young Muslim convert from Saudi at St Mary's church Brighton, England. The young man is wearing a white jumper symbolising new life, whilst the red ribbon symbolises the blood of Christ. Upon his return to Saudi, the young man was murdered for his faith.**

Chapter 13: Facing the Giant - **Fr Zakaria at Life Satellite channel Studios recording one of the most popular TV programs broadcasted in the Middle East (2005).**

But at least this sharper pain provided a distraction from the relentless deeper pain in his kidney. Not only that, the opened cell door allowed for draughts of relatively fresh air to cool the overheated cell.

Unfortunately, in spite of the nurse's best efforts, it was all to no avail. Eventually a doctor had to be called to administer the injection.

Prison life became predictable through daily routines. For Zakaria, this meant following the disciplines of his priestly office. Each day commenced with worship, prayer and Scripture reading. After a break, this ordered activity was repeated. In the evenings the entire group of Christians participated in Bible studies of the New Testament books of Ephesians, Philippians and Hebrews.

At the conclusion of the evening studies, Zakaria would pray and fall asleep about midnight. For forty-four days until October 16 the personal and corporate routine continued.

The cell block in which the Christians were incarcerated was known as 'the trial'. Allegedly prison authorities reserved it to accommodate the most dangerous and uncontrollable miscreants. Spiritual and physical darkness pervaded its precincts. Frequently in the absence of a reliable electricity supply, prisoners were literally kept in the dark from 4.00p.m. daily. All living creatures, even hardened criminals, long for light. In 'the trial' this was frequently denied.

The height of each cell was just 1.8 metres. This was an additional challenge for Zakaria who was 1.83 metres tall. Lack of ventilation and lighting with insufficient room to move was bad enough. But what really troubled the prisoners, was a lack of news regarding the welfare of their families from whom they had been removed. Whenever prisoners sought personal news, answers were frequently provided via prison warders. Subsequent cross checking revealed that mostly all they received were lies.

Initially only occupants from one single cell at a time were allowed out for exercise. This was later amended to permit the inmates of two then four cells outside simultaneously. But communication and socialisation among prisoners were guardedly restricted.

Only one class of individuals had unrestricted visitation rights to each cell, even though it was at the risk of their own lives. This was the clouds of well nourished, oversized mosquitoes, which bred undisturbed in uncovered sewers outside the prison walls. Their blood, stolen in battles with desperate prisoners, was splattered across the walls and doors of each cell.

Prisoners, irritated by the constant swarms of mosquitoes, asked prison staff to fumigate their cells with insecticide. Eventually prison authorities granted their request. Spraying began each night at 10.00 p.m. Prisoners waited outside their cells while spraying was in progress. Then they returned and cells were immediately locked down again. This meant prisoners inhaled as much of the toxic spray as did the mosquitoes. When prisoners asked if they could remain outside their cells for a brief time after the completion of spraying, staff threatened to remove altogether the "privilege" of being sprayed.

As noted earlier, each cell toilet was only a hole in the floor. With three persons to each cramped cell, this scarcely allowed for any personal privacy, not that unwelcome odours could have been confined behind curtains, doors or special partitioning, had there been any.

The only tap for water was situated directly above the excrement encrusted black, stinking hole. Washing food, rinsing dishes or obtaining drinking water was always carried out above that hole - if water was available. Perhaps uniquely in Cairo, it was a one-stop shop location, servicing all personal needs.

Food, if it could be dignified by that name, was brought to each cell in the same old battered buckets which were used to clean the toilets and prison floors. They were originally blue in colour, but had long since become an appropriate shade of brown on the inside. At mealtimes, food-filled buckets were firstly placed in the corridor outside each cell. Flies and cockroaches arrived as uninvited guests to revel in their delicious good fortune. Eventually the buckets' contents were slopped into plastic plates.

Before actually handing the food to the prisoners, guards shouted to draw the inmates' attention to the guards' kindness, in allowing other prison life forms to share the prisoners fare. Nose pickings were an additional treat at no extra expense. Prisoners were never sure what the actual ingredients of their bucket delivered food were supposed to be. In that the delivery system left as much to be desired as that which was served up, the 'food' was usually sluiced straight down the toilet hole without being diverted through prisoners' stomachs. They hungrily subsisted mostly on pieces of bread delivered three times a day

In the earliest days, with such limited space in each overcrowded cell, sleeping became a challenge. If one slept all slept like sardines packed into a can, head to toe. Should one need to roll over, all had to stand, turn and lie back down again. Later, more cells were allocated so that all could enjoy the luxury of having only two inmates per cell. Zakaria was moved from cell 18 to cell 10, leaving Fr Bishoy Yassa and Fr Tadros Malaty to appreciate their extra space. Within each cell conversation became limited. There was only so much two people involuntarily locked into each other's space could explore.

Personal bathing was a luxurious privilege. One cell had been fitted out with two shower heads so the prisoners could bathe two at a time. Again, no privacy was afforded for this activity. A pair of prisoners was to bathe simultaneously within a brief allotted time. Should any exceed that time limit, they were automatically dragged naked back into the corridor.

In this environment of unrelieved stress and distress, inmates' psychological health deteriorated rapidly. With no news of what may have befallen their families and fearful of what the government authorities might be about to visit upon them, deepening depression resulting in attempted suicide became all too common on 'the trial' block.

The Attorney General's Office

At 7.30 am on September 19, after 17 days of being held incommunicado, Zakaria and Athanasius were suddenly called out and handcuffed, ready to be escorted to the office of the Attorney General for a preliminary hearing of their case. To transport these 'dangerous criminals', no security measure was overlooked. Cars were assembled to proceed in convoy. High ranking officials would lead the way, followed by Zakaria and Athanasius, who in turn were followed by an armed escort of five police officers. Bringing up the rear was yet another vehicle filled with the ever present secret police.

With sirens blaring, the procession set off at speed, ignoring all red traffic lights and inconvenience to other drivers. Bystanders could have been forgiven for confusing a possible presidential cavalcade, with a contemporary version of the Keystone Cops.

Upon arrival at the court complex, guards whisked Zakaria and Athanasius up to the eighth floor. A large number of the fundamentalist Islamic organisation, Jamaat El Islamia and the head of the Muslim Brotherhood, Omar El Telmesannee, were already present.

Zakaria learned he was to appear before the chief prosecutor. A Church lawyer had been appointed to assist Zakaria, but he failed to appear until two and a half hours into the five-hour hearing.

In the preliminary stages of the hearing, Zakaria was cross-examined about allegedly baptising 7 Muslim converts. Upon examining the list of names of the aforesaid candidates, Zakaria noted one by the name of 'Hanoom'. This means 'hell'. According to Islamic law, forsaking Islam for another religious faith is apostasy. The penalty for the apostate and for the one who is instrumental in their leaving Islam, is death. The ultimate eternal destination for both is said to be hell. Zakaria saw through the ruse. The list of alleged converts was fictional. Zakaria challenged the prosecutor to present the converts in person to determine whether or not they had been illegally baptised. The challenge was not accepted.

The prosecutor next questioned Zakaria regarding the circumstances surrounding the event of the burnt church in the village of El Khanka. Specifically the prosecutor wanted to know the precise accusation levelled at Zakaria at the El Kanka police station. Zakaria replied that he had been accused of using a microphone without appropriate authorisation and of using a camera to photograph what had happened to the church building. Obviously the government kept a meticulous dossier on Zakaria and anyone else who came to their attention, no matter how trivial the issue.

The prosecutor ground on to examine Zakaria about his allegedly smuggling himself into the El Imam Ali Mosque in Heliopolis after a Friday service, when the leader of the mosque was absent. Even worse, Zakaria was further alleged to have initiated a debate with Muslim worshippers still present in the mosque, during the course of which, he was said to have referred to (incomplete) verses of the Quran and allegedly even distributed Bible tracts to those present.

Zakaria's defence was compellingly simple. "If I had smuggled myself into a mosque full of people, there would have been only two possible outcomes. Either they would have killed me, or they would have filed a complaint at the local police station." As neither of these things had eventuated, obviously the truth was otherwise.

What had happened was that Zakaria had been invited into the mosque by its leaders for a debate about Christianity. The meeting had actually occurred on a Friday night in the presence of many Muslim scholars. Zakaria was seated in a circle among them. They peppered him with many questions. After patiently bearing with their questions and comments for some hours, Zakaria moved to the offensive. He skilfully used verses in the Quran and Hadith (ie the collected sayings and events attributed to the Prophet Mohammad), as well as the teachings of accepted Muslim authorities, to prove the Christian doctrines of the Trinity and the deity of Christ.

> Zakaria was accused of the ultimate crime, evangelising Muslims and thereby inciting religious factionalism.

Eventually debate broke out among the Muslim scholars themselves about what Zakaria had said. Disagreement among them regarding Islamic principles of interpretation and other issues which Zakaria had raised intensified to the degree that they became verbally abusive with one another. Zakaria and his assistant thought it opportune to pick up their shoes and quietly depart. That two Christians should walk into a mosque, be surrounded by hotly debating Muslim scholars and quietly withdraw safely, boarded on the supernatural. Again the prosecutor's accusations fell as victims to truth.

The next item on the prosecutor's agenda, was regarding a book Zakaria had written to explain the Trinity, the association he had formed and the distribution of Christian tracts. Again Zakaria was accused of the ultimate crime, evangelising Muslims and thereby inciting religious factionalism.

At the conclusion of the hearing, Zakaria and Athanasius were driven back to their prison. The route took them near to where Zakaria's family still lived. Not only did they not know their husband and father was passing nearby, since he was forcibly removed from their home, they had received no information whatsoever regarding his whereabouts, what was happening or even why he had been arrested. The family was left bereft, bewildered and confused, consoled only through the tears and visits of many sympathetic friends.

Upon their return to the prison, Saleh, a secret police officer, warned Zakaria not to talk about the investigation. Zakaria would not be so easily intimidated. Back in his cell, as guards listened in, he pretended to reveal all to his fellow inmates and especially that in his opinion, the prosecutor was probably a "just" man.

Later that same night, to report the real truth of what had happened, Zakaria developed a more creative methodology for sharing with all. He made as if he was reading from a book of early church history and retold the entire day long investigation substituting 'Romans' for 'government officials', 'Gentiles' for 'Muslims' and so on. Other prisoners subsequently adopted similar strategies to retell their respective experiences as they occurred.

Death of a President

On October 6 the Christian prisoners were filled with hope and optimism. They had been advised to expect a visit from Bishop Samuel, accompanied by representatives from the Ministry of Justice and the association of prison management. In anticipation of an opportunity to speak on their own behalf to the delegation, the prisoners had elected as representatives, Bishop Beemen, Fr Tadros Malaty and Mr Bastaoros. All hoped that the visit would result in their being released. To their great disappointment, without explanation, the planned visit was postponed.

The next day on the morning of October 7, the officer in charge of the entire prison, gave instructions to open slightly all cell doors, so that all inmates could simultaneously clearly hear an important announcement. Prisoners were warned to remain silent and not to comment on the announcement. Then came the news. "The President of Egypt has died and martial law has been declared. Lock all cells."

That brief announcement raised more questions than it provided answers. Did the President die of natural causes or had he been assassinated? Had there been a revolution? What part if any did the army play? What about the Islamist's Jamaat El Islamia or other similarly oriented groups? What was the condition of their families during the state of emergency? When if ever, might they now expect to be freed? It took a week for reports to filter through to the prisoners about what had really happened.

On October 6, during a military parade in Cairo, four army personnel had broken free from the procession. Armed with loaded automatic weapons, they had attacked the official viewing stand. In the ensuing fire fight, many had been wounded and President Sadat had been assassinated. The lieutenant in charge of the hit squad had shouted out, "I am Khalid al Islambuli. I have killed Pharaoh and I do not fear death." All the assassins were members of an underground movement appropriately named, 'Jihad.' They were led by Abdul Salaam Faraj. They validated their action by declaring Sadat's regime as un-Islamic, thus making it a lawful duty to kill its leader. Sadat's gamble in recognising Israel had cost him his life. Vice President Hosni Mubarak was immediately elevated to replace President Sadat.

CHAPTER 8

HOPE DELAYED

Light Relief

Even on the darkest nights distant starlight pierces that darkness. It is similar with life's blackest experiences. Prison life was tough. But distraction and relief turned up in the oddest ways. Prison guard, Abdul El Ghony was one such source.

After completing the obligatory ablutions required before each of the five times daily Muslim prayer sessions, Mr Ghony noticed he was still wearing his watch. That meant he had not washed his wrist under where the watch was. According to some Muslim traditions, should just one hair remain unwashed, preparation for prayer was incomplete. The effects of such prayer would be nullified and merit otherwise accrued from the prayer would be discredited. Some Muslims reportedly believe that if just one of the five times daily prayer is missed, the penalty is 5,000 years in hell! Proper prayer preparation is therefore regarded as a serious matter.

Abdul El Ghony knew he faced a serious problem. He would have to repeat in its entirety, the ritual washing - minus the watch. The question was, where could he safely leave a wristwatch unguarded in the midst of a prison filled with desperate criminals? A compliant cat which just happened to be passing by, could possibly be Allah's answer to the predicament.

Seizing the cat, Abdul Ghony fastened his watch around the cat's neck. He next rewashed himself in the appropriate manner and started to pray. The cat however, was obviously unconcerned about its own eternal destiny. Nor did it seem to be a sincerely cooperative participant in Ghony's prayer planning. As Ghony prostrated himself in prayer, the cat chose that precise moment to abscond! The process of prayer, once commenced, was too important to be interrupted by any distraction. Finding the cat and retrieving the watch, would just have to wait. Besides, it was unlikely that the cat could conceal itself for long or escape from the prison precincts, any more than its human counterparts could. Let prayer continue.

Upon its completion, Ghony searched high and low throughout the entire prison for that cat and his watch. He even administered just retribution on every member of its species whenever he found one. Considering them co-conspirators, he unleashed vicious kicks to the appropriate parts of their anatomy. Alas, it was all to no avail. The feline felon had executed a timely escape and was never seen again, much to the amusement of inmates who had watched the drama unfold.

As a practising Muslim, Ghony knew that not only was the ritual washing which preceded prayer important, so was the covering clothing which one wore. Once when guard Ghony heard one of the priests singing a Christian hymn during his carefully timed shower, Ghony raced to find a Bishop. To this ecclesiastical authority, in a state of shocked panic he sputtered, "Bishop, your priest is praying naked." If cross-cultural misconceptions are rife even among people whose language and nationality are the same by birth, what hope is there for an outsider?

After three weeks of internment, prison authorities permitted prisoners' families to deposit monies to be credited to their respective relatives' prison accounts. Prisoners in turn, could access the funds to buy biscuits, cheese and especially cigarettes. Cigarettes were the unofficial black market currency of the prison. As each new shift of guards came on duty, Zakaria, a non-smoker, would present them with a new pack of cigarettes. This bought favour from the guards. In return for the cigarettes, the guards allowed Zakaria's cell door to remain open a little longer than necessary, so that he could enjoy the privilege of additional fresh air, not that any air within the prison was that fresh in terms of being unpolluted. Abdul Ghony, also profiting from the proffered cigarettes, would leave Zakaria's cell unlocked on occasion. He even allowed Zakaria extra time in the shower and with the additional luxury of showering alone. Ghony, a simple man of unquestioning faith, was quite impressed by Zakaria, because that name is mentioned five times in the sacred text of his Quran.

A Friend from the Past

On Zakaria's first day in El Marg, he was visited by the chief officer of the prison. Upon learning the name of his new prisoner, this officer next inquired as to whether or not there was more than one priest in Cairo named Zakaria Botross. Zakaria assured him that he was the only one of that name. Without further comment the officer departed.

A few days later the same officer returned, this time to inquire whether or not Zakaria knew a Christian medical doctor by the name of Ramses. Zakaria replied in the affirmative. To reassure himself that Zakaria was who he claimed to be and that he was telling the truth, the officer then asked Zakaria to tell him where Dr Ramses worked and to name the doctor's wife. Zakaria replied telling the officer where the doctor worked and that his wife was named Samira.

Sure now that he was speaking to the right person, the chief officer then recounted how he had met Zakaria years previously, in a private meeting at the doctor's home. At the time he was in charge of the secret police in the district of New Cairo. As a part of his responsibilities, he would attend Zakaria's weekly meetings in St Mark's Church hall and file reports of his observations. There he had seen miracles of supernatural healings.

This secret police officer had a personal problem he was desperate to solve. His son was suffering with leukaemia. Through the prayers of Zakaria, healing might be found. But he was too fearful to bring his son to a public event in a Christian church. That course of action could create too many professional and social problems for him. So, like Nicodemus of New Testament fame, he planned an alternate approach.

His wife, also a medical doctor, worked with Dr Ramses. Through her a private meeting was arranged in the good doctor's home with Zakaria, the local head of the secret police, his veiled wife and their son. During the course of that memorable meeting, Zakaria prayed for the child. He was healed. That father could never forget what had happened through Zakaria's ministry. So grateful did he remain, that he also allowed Zakaria's cell door to remain open on occasion, to suck in some of the much desired fresh air. He extended other small favours within the limits of the prison system by passing on family news. A friend through a deed became a friend in a time of need, even though the Quran explicitly forbids Muslims to be friends with infidel Christians, Jews or others.

New Address - Another Prison

On the morning of Friday October 16, the second day in power of the new President of Egypt, Hosni Mubarak, the 32 prisoners in Zakaria's group were handed their belongings and squeezed into a single VW Kombi van. Zakaria was given the responsibility by his colleagues to work out where they were going, by observing their route through the vehicle's back window. They were very relieved to pass by El Kalaa prison which had an exceptionally bad reputation.

Driving through New Cairo, their hopes rose with the possibility they might be being taken to the High Court to be released. No such good fortune. Their spirits sank as they passed on by. Then they were petrified when, as they were crossing the El Geeza Bridge, the vehicle following the prisoners' van indicated they were about to turn left. This would have had them proceeding to either Nagaa Hamadee or El Wadee El Gadeed Prisons, either of which would have indicated a long stay behind bars. All breathed a sigh of relief when the van's driver opted not to leave the road on which he was already driving.

Then, at the intersection which led to El Fayoom Prison, their van stopped and remained there for 30 minutes. The prisoners were devastated at the prospect of what awaited them in what appeared about to be their new location. Its reputation had been established long before their arrival. But then to the prisoners' ecstatic delight, their transport moved off again, this time along the Cairo Alexandria Road. They realised at last that they had to be heading for the Leeman Wadi El Natroon Prison. Of all the possibilities this was the best outcome.

Upon arrival, after being unpacked from their extremely overcrowded vehicle, all of their party, to their grateful delight, were permitted to enjoy fresh air and blue sky while sitting in the prison grounds, before being locked away once more. They were then taken inside to a large 12 x 8 metre room. Its door was made of bars rather than solid steel. This meant fresh air was accessible. Not only that, it had a 12 x 50 centimetre window which let in light as well. Comparatively, this was luxury indeed. It was also to be their home for the next 35 days till November 20.

Of particular pleasure to the imprisoned Christian community, was the fact that they were all together again in the one block. They could talk and encourage one another. The prison officers were also more kindly disposed toward their charges. A few of them, namely Bishops Benjamin, Tadros, Bemoa and Frs Bishoy, Yassa, Bishoy of Bor Saeed and Zakaria, commenced a total fast abstaining from all food and liquid for three days, which Zakaria repeated twice more in the following weeks.

Court investigations recommenced by processing Frs Basilius Sidrak, Philipos, Bishop Benjamin and others. Gradually conditions for the prisoners also improved. Food was allowed to be brought in each Tuesday and Saturday via Girgis Eskander, a delegate from the Patriarch. Prisoners were also permitted to receive from their families a few letters. From October 23 they began to receive newspapers as well.

On October 24, Zakaria received a bouquet of flowers and a present for his birthday from his family. From then on, birthdays, ordination anniversaries and any other special occasions which could be thought up, all became reasons for community celebrations.

Back on the Home front

While Zakaria was adjusting to prison life, and the constant close pressure of his colleagues, his distressed family was struggling with his unrelieved absence. They didn't know if they would ever see him again. His wife wrote many letters to the newly appointed president, Hosni Mubarak, pleading for her husband's release or at least permission to visit him. Her letter writing, straight from the heart, was an attempt to touch that of the President:

> I beg you from a torn and painful heart. I beg you with a soul that is brought to dust as a result of my difficult circumstances. I beg you that you release my husband whom we have not seen for two months. I trust your justice and I know that you are aware of my husband's surpassing faithfulness to God, our country and to all people. He has no other purpose in life except to please God. He walks according to God's commands.... I am persuaded that God will reveal to you my husband's innocence and his love for our nation. I want to let you know that my children's hearts are destroyed because of their father's absence.... I hope you have compassion on our little child, Peter, who goes without his meals on most days, to the point that his health has deteriorated. I hope you allow us to visit my husband at your soonest opportunity.

The son Peter, to whom the letter refers, was 7 years of age at that time. On October 28, with maturity way beyond his years, he also wrote to the President as follows:

> I congratulate your honour for the new role of Presidency and I implore your gracious heart that comprehends the love of a father for a son. Would you allow me to visit my father because I miss him so much and for two months I have been deprived of his tender affections? Have compassion on my little heart that bleeds from the hurt of separation. I also haven't been able to study.

Meanwhile hundreds of kilometres away, approximately halfway between Cairo and Alexandria, in El Leeman Prison, Zakaria was quite unaware of all this letter writing activity. His diary records the measured pace of regulated prison life:

> My daily program in El Leeman Prison consists of prayers from a prayer book, breakfast, followed by a recess from 9.00 to 11.00a.m. We have a group Bible study from the book of Genesis, led by Bishop Bishoy. Fr Tadros Malaty next leads a Bible study from the book of Ezekiel. I then pray the sixth and the ninth hour prayers and have lunch. We have a break from 3.00 to 4.00p.m. and then pray again. I then read the newspaper, which is followed by a message from Bishop Beemen from one of the New Testament epistles. We finish the day in prayer and worship.

The diary reads like a continuous Christian convention, but the harsh realities within the context of prison life, reveal something quite different.

Government Hospitality

Like all prisons in Egypt, El Leeman was very dirty. The toilets lived down to normal expectations. Thirty adults were squeezed into the same cell with decrepit, worn out triple-tier bunks. This was no five-star tourist experience on the banks of the Nile in the land of the ancient Pharaohs.

While no visitors were allowed from outside the prison, there were plenty of uninvited visitors already resident in the prison. Bunks piled on one another were held shakily together by hollow metal pieces. In these dark cavities were domiciled plagues of multiplying cockroaches. Zakaria, precariously occupying a top bunk, restricted their inquisitive meanderings across his person, by plugging the open ends of the pipes with crumpled newspapers. He preferred his own to their nocturnal company.

Mice movements were not so easily restricted. On one occasion, one of the inmates in their cell suddenly awoke screaming with fright and pain because a mouse had drawn blood while nibbling his toe.

The iron barred door did let in fresh air, for which all were grateful. But it did not restrain the cold as winter approached. Water was scarce. It was available only three times a day. Physical conditions were difficult but manageable. More challenging were the social and spiritual states imposed upon the group through overcrowding.

Zakaria felt in control of neither his time nor his space. Everything of necessity was shared. In a broader sense, there was no room for individual tastes, tendencies or preferences. As the group settled into a routine and environment comparatively more comfortable than in their previous prison, worship weakened. Communal prayer lost its sharpened edge of urgency. It assumed more predictable habitual forms. Interpersonal problems arose among individuals unnecessarily straining relationships. But none of these issues compared to the behaviour of prison staff.

The chief officer of the prison set the standard by violently beating prisoners in front of the others, probably to intimidate all of them into quiescent submission. Guards, without warning, would often suddenly invade the cell to search through every possession of every inmate.

On one occasion, Bishop Beemen had some design drawings for a sound system he was developing for his parish church. Concerned lest they be discovered, he asked Zakaria for advice. Zakaria advised him to put the papers under the pile of rubbish in the bin.

Two hours later, a spot search by the guards uncovered the drawings. Bishop Beemen was summoned to the prison office to account for the find. He advised the investigating officer that responsibility for the papers was not his, but more could be learned by their questioning Zakaria.

Zakaria was aware that ad hoc inquisitions were taken quite seriously, as if they had the authority of formal trials. Nevertheless, for this hearing, Zakaria appeared bedecked in his nightgown! When asked what he knew about the offending papers, Zakaria boldly replied that they had been thrown into the bin so that the search party would not find them and make a big fuss over nothing. For good measure, he assured the authorities that neither he nor his cellmates were really that interested in designing and installing a sound system for the prison.

Having satisfied the inquiry on that score, Zakaria was next questioned regarding his clothing. The officers' honour was affronted by Zakaria's grossly informal and inappropriate attire for such a serious occasion. Zakaria turned the tables by pointing out that the prison was really home to all the inmates. They lived there all the time. In one's home the dress code of informality was entirely appropriate. The guards, who daily came and went, were in fact visitors to the prisoners' home, so all was in order.

Joys of Communal Living

Not everything was unpleasant in El Leeman. Compared with their previous place of incarceration, they did have better air to breathe, light by which to see and mobility. There were also the prayer meetings at night and the theological discussions which Zakaria could enjoy with his clerical friends, Frs Tadros and Loka and Bishops Benjamin, Beemen and Bishoy. Such discussion groups sharpened their theological positions and enriched their fellowship.

Leeman prison also provided Zakaria with opportunities to serve his Christian brothers in practical ways. There were dishes to wash after meals, toilets to clean and hair to be cut. All prisoners owned white underwear, which could be lumped together in a confused pile when returned from the laundry. Zakaria solved the identification problem by becoming an adept amateur tailor for the group. He carefully extracted multicoloured threads from his towel and sewed each person's initials onto their underwear.

Prison visits

Zakaria's family continued to suffer severe distress. They still had no idea of when or if they would see him again. A kindly priest, Fr Youhanna Bakee visited the family each week to pray and give encouragement. Others gave what support they could. But none could adequately console the family for the sudden loss of their beloved husband and father.

Violet in particular felt lost. She customarily consulted Zakaria on everything, always depending on him to make the final decision. Oldest child Janet now married to Samir, moved back to the family home to provide support. The extended family was spooked into suspecting that the police may have bugged their home with secret listening devices. To avoid inadvertently revealing personal information, they devised codes by which they frequently reminded one another of the possibility of being overheard.

When the family learned of Zakaria's deprivations in prison, Violet refused normal meals and slept on the floor to identify with her husband's sufferings. Likewise, youngest child Peter refused to eat anything at all until he was reassured that at least his father had been provided with similar food in jail.

Ben's sufferings were of a different order but nevertheless related to his father's imprisonment. With Zakaria's movements confined to prison precincts, obviously he would have no use for his car. Ben sought and gained permission to use it himself. Ever the tearaway, on his first outing with his best friend Adel, he managed to smash into a bus injuring his friend, himself, the car and his reputation as a brilliant driver, not quite yet up to Grand Prix standards.

Zakaria and his companions were returned to El Marg Prison on November 20. When they arrived they were allocated a freshly painted cell which measured 25 x 10 metres. It had large barred windows with glass to keep out the winter cold. For the first two weeks the prisoners were provided with mattresses on the floor, after which they were given clean beds! Zakaria was able to make a tiny room for himself by hanging blankets between the beds.

In this newly restored environment, the guards also appeared to have been renovated. They were kinder. They even allowed the group to remain outside their cell till almost 4.00p.m. each afternoon. Prisoners were given time for physical exercise and reading. They took turns in leading Bible studies in the prison grounds.

The family naturally wanted to see Zakaria again. But even when they discovered his whereabouts, to visit him was no easy matter. The first time they tried, the prison authorities left them standing outside the prison for the entire visitation period. They begged the authorities to allow them just to wave to him. They could see him smiling and waving at them and even from that distance noticed he was much thinner. They had difficulty at first recognising this slimmed down version.

Young Peter managed to slip between a soldier's legs. He raced to embrace his father regardless of whether or not such an act had official sanction. The boy sobbed uncontrollably. He had missed his father so much.

The second visit was a slight improvement. Members of the family could converse with Zakaria through iron bars and from behind screens. Eventually they were able to sit with him in the prison office for up to 15 minutes at a time.

During these visits, Zakaria and his family would both bring boxes of tissues into the visitation room. This was not just to soak up copious tears shed by all. At the start of the visit, both boxes were placed on the table between visited and visitors. By the end of the session, the boxes had been surreptitiously exchanged. In this way more intimate family communications were effected. At the bottom of Zakaria's box underneath all the tissues, the family found his diary notes, letters to each family member and devotional meditations he had compiled. One of these was appropriately titled, 'Embracing the Cross.' Its tender sensitivity had the effect of reducing to tears all who read it.

Hope after Hope

Within this improved situation, prisoners' hopes rose as they began to speculate on the possibility of their imminent release. On December 12 the El Ahram newspaper reported that the government had decided to abolish decisions handed down on September 5 by former President Sadat, prior to his assassination. Specifically the edict stated:

> The judicial court in its meeting yesterday presided over by Councillor Saad Abo Owf, issued a decision to suspend the execution of the decisions made by President El Sadat, number 493 for the year 81, issued on the fifth of September.

Three days later, on December 15, news was received of 58 prisoners scheduled for release over two days. Within another 2 days, on December 17, the inmates awoke to the exhilarating news of a broadcast originating from London, that said 297 individuals who had been arrested for religious reasons, were about to be released.

In a state of almost euphoric disbelief everyone excitedly got up, got dressed, packed their meagre possessions and readied themselves for release. But when the daily newspaper arrived, their hopes were dashed. The reports had been false - the outcome of a misprint.

Later that day, Zakaria's family were permitted to make their third visit. They arrived at 1.00p.m. Although the day had been a rapid rollercoaster of emotional highs and lows, the end of the ride was coloured with a little happiness. It was son Peter's eighth birthday. Songs were sung. Candles were lit and extinguished, along with the hope of imminent release of Zakaria and his companions.

Life in El Marg resumed its steady pace. There were the repeated disappointments of waiting for confirmation of definite release which never came. But this was counterbalanced by the opportunities to build friendships, serve others and for Zakaria in particular, to research the early Church Fathers' comments on the book of Romans. He also used the time for detailed study of the Old Testament prophetic book - Ezekiel.

Innovative Witnessing

Zakaria's family was now able to send food weekly for his subgroup of 8 persons. They also often sent food for 130 non-Christians in the prison. Zakaria developed other innovative ways of reaching out and testifying to his Christian faith.

One non-Christian prisoner spent hours playing a board game called Backgammon. Zakaria requested that he be taught the game as well. When he had mastered it, he bargained - one board game for a discussion of the gospel of Jesus. The man loved the game and playing against Zakaria. Zakaria in turn loved his 'captive' audience of one.

To demonstrate the love of Jesus in practical ways, Zakaria's group continued to send food to other cells. On one occasion when Bishop Beemen went to a cell block to deliver food parcels, he left minus his wallet. Upon realising what had happened, he requested permission from the guard to talk with the suspected thief.

"Son did I harm you in any way?" asked the Bishop.

"Of course not, Sir. You are very kind to us," the thief replied.

"So why did you reward me with evil?"

"Evil? No way, Sir. God forbid."

"You stole my wallet, didn't you?"

"Yes, I did."

"Isn't that evil?"

"No, it's an idle hand that is evil, Sir!"

This line of argument would seem strange to Christian ears. Christian theology teaches that wrongdoing or sin, is always the result of the sinner exercising freedom of choice. As such, that one is personally responsible. But from a Muslim perspective, Allah is the first cause of all things. Therefore he may be persuader and deceiver. The hapless sinner is not responsible. Allah does what he wills. The sinner however will receive his just desserts in this life and the next. In the case of the thief, the application of Shariah law is to cut off the idle hand which was the instrument of the crime (Sura 5:38).

As a bewildered Bishop retreated, Zakaria, who had been present, ever eager to learn, asked the thief about the practice of his profession. Specifically he wanted to know how something could be stolen from a person without that person's being aware of what had happened. The thief offered to demonstrate his craft on Zakaria's person.

Zakaria accepted the challenge. He was wearing his priestly robe which had a small pocket at the top and another larger one at the side in which he kept his own wallet. To make it doubly difficult for the thief, Zakaria put his hand in his pocket and tightly held his wallet, while he transfixed the thief with his unflinching gaze. Within seconds, the thief suddenly announced that the deed was done.

Withdrawing the wallet and holding it up for the thief to see, Zakaria pointed out that the wallet was still in his possession. The thief laughed and invited Zakaria to look at what was balancing on his left shoulder. Sure enough, there was a small cake of soap which the thief had removed from Zakaria's upper pocket and then left it on his shoulder to demonstrate his art.

Although Zakaria never discovered how it was done, his curiosity was stirred even further. Wanting to know more about how these men lived by their wits and their hands, which moved faster either than the eye could see or the brain could comprehend, Zakaria asked another practitioner as to his modus operandi.

This fellow advised that his main tool in trade was his own spittle. As he approached a likely victim, he would 'accidentally' spit on their shoulder. Then, with flourishes of profuse apologies, he would immediately make a great fuss of cleaning the dribbling saliva from the innocent's clothing using his own handkerchief. Duly distracted, the person's wallet was cleanly extracted without the victim's noticing it. The thief forthwith made a clean getaway by diving into the ever flowing river of ceaselessly passing humanity, so characteristic of many Egyptian public spaces.

CHAPTER 9

FREEDOM AT LAST

On July 17 1982, the chief officer of the prison visited Zakaria to congratulate him on the news that he would be released the following day. At first Zakaria didn't dare believe him. Previously this officer had informed Zakaria that he and Bishop Benjamin would either be executed or sentenced to spend many years in prison. In spite of Zakaria's doubts, the officer persisted in urging Zakaria to treat the news as highly confidential until its later public announcement.

Unusually for Zakaria, he wept throughout the night. His fellow prisoners were concerned for and alarmed about him. Zakaria was not upset for himself. Who would be, at the thought of hopefully vacating such miserably restrictive conditions? His distress was occasioned by the thought of those he was about to leave behind. One of his fellow priests had just received news of the birth of his first child. When for instance, would this new father ever be able to see and hold his baby? Each had similarly heart-wrenching personal stories.

After a long and anxious night, prison officers came for Zakaria, took him from the confinement of his ward-like cell and escorted him from the prison precincts, through the gates, out to where his son-in-law Samir waited to take him home. After 318 days and nights, he was free at last. A huge celebration with family and friends, as only Egyptians could conceive, awaited him at home.

Although the physical restraints of prison life were a thing of the past, for the time being Zakaria's freedoms and privileges weren't entirely restored. The government's release order contained a condition that no priest thus freed was to be permitted to return to his previous post. Hence, every priest was reappointed to resume ministry in parishes other than where they had previously been serving. This was a typical example of government interference and control over affairs of the Christian community. However, in Zakaria's case, there was an additional restraint.

The church declined to reinstate him to ministry and priestly privileges. Within the ecclesiastical hierarchies, there was greater reluctance to forgive or to forbear than in the hostile Muslim government. Some of his clerical opponents preferred to remain fiercely opposed to Zakaria's total restoration, even though there seemed little if anything he had done wrong. As an omen of future hope, at least one parish priest had a change of heart. He began sending greetings and a loaf of special bread associated with communion each week.

Life Lessons

Life in prison had been tough and challenging. But like King David of ancient Israel, Zakaria understood, that irrespective of physical circumstances, God was working out his purposes (Psalm 57:2). He believed all things were meant to serve God (Psalm 119:91), that the Lord works out everything for his own ends (Psalm 16:4) and that ultimately those ends are "for the good of those who love him, who have been called according to his purpose" (Romans 8:28). With this attitude, Zakaria accepted that his 'cell days' had taught him invaluable life lessons. These included:

1. The priority of prayer.

    With little to do all day but pray, he grew to enjoy being in the presence of God. He prayed using the guidance of a prayer book. He conversed freely with God. He meditated on Scripture throughout the day. He worshipped the Lord with a contrite and humbled spirit.

2. Submission to the will of God.

   He had to surrender everything most dear to him, family, friends and ministry. He experienced the death of his own will.

3. Preparation to meet the Lord.

   Prison often seemed like a rehearsal for death. He often wondered, particularly through the long and lonely nights, what would be the effects on his family, if his next visitor was not the police officers or prison guards, but the executioner or the Angel of death itself.

> **Although the physical restraints of prison life were a thing of the past, for the time being Zakaria's freedoms and privileges weren't entirely restored. ... The church declined to reinstate him to ministry and priestly privileges.**

4. Thanksgiving.

   If, as Jesus taught, God is aware of the fate of single sparrows and knows the number of hairs on each person's head (Luke 12: 6-7), then he surely exercises care and control over the smallest detail of one's life and therefore he should be thanked in all circumstances (1 Thessalonians 5:18).

5. Love for enemies.

   Through trials and experience, he eventually learned to love his enemies and to pray for those who treated him unjustly and harshly (Matthew 5:44).

6. Appreciation for his family.

   He had time to consider and really appreciate his wife's labour of love in caring for the family, especially in his many and prolonged absences. In this, he was also reminded of his own sacred responsibilities in caring and providing for his family and for raising his children in the ways of God.

7. God's sovereignty.

   While the world related President Sadat's assassination to Islamic fundamentalists, for Zakaria it was a demonstration of God's might, authority and power, in overthrowing a President who had ordered the arrest of him and his colleagues and who had in all likelihood intended to have them executed. Only the Living One holds the keys to life and death (Revelation 1:18). His will irresistibly overrules all (Revelation 3:7).

New Beginnings

The end of prison was the beginning of new life for the family. During incarceration, God had specifically spoken to Zakaria regarding the discharge of his responsibilities within the family. The Biblical passage which had the greatest impact was in Paul's letter to Timothy:

> If anyone does not provide for his relatives and especially for his immediate family, he has denied the faith and is worse than an unbeliever (1 Timothy 5:8).

Upon release he took extra time to rebuild carefully relationships within the home. He made a covenant to invest quality time with his children. He even took time to teach those board games he had learnt in prison. He took the family on frequent trips to the seaside city of Alexandria and other nearby destinations.

He also adopted a different attitude toward correction and discipline of the children. He asked for forgiveness from his eldest son Feyez and his third son Ben, for the way in which he had disciplined them in the past. Feyez was shocked that his own father would do such a thing. It was so out of character. It was also quite contrary to any known precedent in the culture. Parents never apologised for anything to children. But these bold actions meant that Zakaria became first friend and then hero, greatly respected and admired by all his family.

Like many before him, Zakaria's wholehearted commitment to ministry, along with his willingness to respond to the many demands made upon him, left little time to be with his family. As the children grew, they came to realise that their father was well known throughout Egypt, by Christians and Muslims alike. He freely gave himself to those in need. Often his sleep was interrupted by people wanting his help to solve their problems. He was available, day and night, especially to help parents whose children were considering converting to Islam, which was always a pressure on the Christian community.

As would any child, his son Ben longed to spend time talking with his father. He even waited up till late at night for Zakaria's return, from pastoral visits, preaching or his endless travel. A late supper was the only opportunity Ben could find to worm his way into his father's presence, to talk over all the things growing children delight in discussing with seemingly all knowing fathers. These were the times Zakaria was not the stern paternal disciplinarian. He metamorphosed instead into a sensitive counsellor and life coach.

With family relationships back on track, it was time to resume ministry, restricted though it was. For Zakaria, this meant a return to his beloved priority of making disciples. Even though he had been removed through imprisonment, the many small groups he had established, had flourished, reproduced and multiplied. In this way, many were affected who otherwise would have been beyond reach. Lives were changed permanently.

In one clandestine Bible study group, a young 13-year-old gave his life to Jesus. He immediately phoned his girlfriend from a nearby corner store, advised her of his decision and terminated their relationship. Still today that one serves in a full-time Christian ministry capacity.

Zakaria had previously decided not to have television in the home. This decision had to be revisited when a friend donated a TV and VCR to the family. The boys were very excited, at least for a whole hour. Then Zakaria informed them he was going to lock the TV away. They would only be allowed to watch Christian videos or educational programs. Later there would be one exception - football (soccer).

Father and sons eventually watched matches together. Unfortunately his ever increasing knowledge of Christian theology and Islam, did not include the world game. He frustrated his children by asking questions every few minutes about what was happening. At the tensest times, the penalty shootouts, when his son Peter was on his knees praying aloud for God's intervention on behalf of his favourite team, Zakaria seemed hardly moved by such passionate expressions of spirituality.

Inquisitions

Throughout 1982-87 dialogues continued with the church authorities, in the hope of effecting reconciliation specifically with the Pope of the Coptic Church. Zakaria regularly presented himself at a monastery to be examined by a committee presided over by two bishops. It was appointed to discuss and resolve points of theological differences and tensions. The issue of 'salvation in a moment' was high on the agenda.

> Zakaria's revolutionary return to the earliest formulations of the doctrine, represented a huge challenge to the church - or more particularly, to its ranked clergy.

Zakaria had published a book to expound on the subject of salvation, as he had come to understand it, from his study of the Bible and examination of the writings and preaching of the early Church Fathers. In the intervening centuries, the simplicity of salvation through faith alone had been obscured, if not lost, through encrustations of church deliberations and decisions. Zakaria's revolutionary return to the earliest formulations of the doctrine, represented a huge challenge to the church - or more particularly, to its ranked clergy.

While the issue of salvation was fundamental, significant and serious, other issues were hardly so. When questioned by a bishop regarding assurance of a heavenly abode beyond death, Zakaria replied that 'by God's grace' he was certain that would be his ultimate destination. Immediately the bishop drew the attention of the committee to the fact that Zakaria was reliant upon God's grace, rather than his mercy. The bishop was adamant that Zakaria must agree that he would be heaven bound only by God's mercy. Zakaria obstinately refused to concede the point. The argument intensified. Ultimately Zakaria gathered his belongings, left the meeting and returned to Cairo. It was left to a more moderately tolerant member of the committee to restore order.

In 1985, the Pope was finally released from the monastic exile imposed upon him by the government. He was allowed to return to the patriarchate of Cairo to resume his papal responsibilities. Church authorities requested Zakaria to supervise security for the Pope's special service in the cathedral. With a trusted youth team, Zakaria processed in excess of 10,000 personal identity cards belonging to those who wanted to see the Pope and attend the service. This menial task became the first step toward Zakaria's reconciliation within the church.

In 1987 at the feast of Pentecost, the Pope asked Zakaria to pray with him in a public service. On that very day, Zakaria was at last recommissioned to minister at St George's church in Mansheyet El Tahreer, about 15 minutes travelling time from where he and his family were living.

CHAPTER 10

PEOPLE, POLICE AND PRISONS

As soon as Zakaria settled in at St George's, he began special Saturday night meetings. In huge numbers people flocked to hear him. The church could not contain them. An audiovisual system was purchased and installed, so that anyone within 50 metres of the church could join in. People then packed adjoining halls as well as nearby Christian homes. As Zakaria preached through the book of Genesis, thousands of people turned up each Saturday night, to listen intently to God's word expounded by this Spirit-anointed preacher.

Discipleship through small groups flourished throughout the church. Leaders whom Zakaria had trained while under suspension, found a spiritual home and a welcome to minister to the ever increasing crowds. Revival and growth also broke out among the youth.

Personal visitation in Christian homes became very time consuming. To ensure other aspects of ministry were not neglected, Zakaria trained teams for ministry in hospitals, orphanages and for special cases of bereavement. Additionally, each month he personally met with many hundreds of individuals, shepherding and mentoring their growth in God. Each received his exclusive attention for 30 minutes. Once more the demands of ministry were drawing him away from availability to his family.

Muslim Ministry

Zakaria did not go seeking Muslims to whom he could preach. They came to him. They seemed as drawn as the hungry are to good food. A tough, assertive, veiled Muslim woman, who was a school principal, was a typical example of the dangers of ministry to Muslims in an Islamic dominated country.

This woman, like many of her coreligionists, hated and persecuted Christians. That is an experience common to many non-Muslims, wherever Islam has taken control of various countries during the almost 14 centuries of its existence. But God touched this woman through the integrity and witness of a few Christian teachers at the school of which she was in charge. Her search for truth began. Through processes needfully left unwritten, eventually she was introduced to ultimate Truth - Jesus.

Unfortunately zeal exceeded wisdom. Her testimony was tape recorded. In that testimony she innocently named others who had helped her along the way of her spiritual search. One of the tapes inevitably found its way into the hands of the ever vigilant secret police. Typically, their response was swift and brutal. The details of their dealings with just one named individual need suffice as a record of what happened to many others.

This man, better left unnamed, was abducted by the secret police and taken to a deserted house which was supposedly haunted. In cases in which a Muslim chooses to leave the coercive control of Islam, that person, as well as any others who may have been involved, place their lives in danger of legally protected retaliation from relatives of the 'apostate' or from officers of the State.

The victim was firstly savagely beaten and then submerged in water up to his neck. He was left in that state for 3 days. This might literally be described as a softening up process for what was to follow. At the end of 3 days, he was removed and strapped into a metal chair through which an electric current was passed, but not of sufficient strength to kill him instantly. Physical reaction to electrocution is better left to the imagination or to medical texts. This inhumane process was repeated many times. Finally the man was dumped in a deserted alley, left just alive, to serve as a warning to others foolish enough to witness about Jesus to Muslims searching for real peace and truth about God.

Many practising Christians as well as converts from Islam, suffered horrific persecution for their faith from the secret police in Cairo. Their stories, for the time being, must remain untold. Many have been cast out, bereft of family or friends. There is no one to record their name or to shout their fame. But their day will come.

> Zakaria did not go seeking Muslims to whom he could preach. They came to him.

They are already known in heaven. Like those listed as heroes of the faith in Hebrews 11, some of these also have *"faced jeers and flogging, while others were chained and put in prison...."* (Hebrews 11:36). *They also have overcome "by the blood of the lamb and the word of their testimony; they did not love their lives so much as to shrink from death"* (Revelation 12:11). The afflictions they have suffered on earth are not to be compared with the glory to come, as God grants to each a place of highest honour.

Conflict Resumes

Inevitably the secret police caught up with Zakaria as well. Weapons had allegedly been found at the Adam mosque not far from St George's church. Adel El Nozahey, a police officer, phoned Zakaria and ordered him to cease preaching. This officer thought he could restore control over the suburb if he could stop the growing Christian movement. Zakaria requested that Nozahey issue his order via the Pope, who alone had the authority to close down Christian meetings in Coptic churches. The police officer was furious at Zakaria's refusal to be intimidated by him. He told Zakaria he would pay for his intransigence. Zakaria asked Nozahey if he was making a threat.

When the officer replied in the affirmative, Zakaria coolly advised him the conversation had been recorded. Nozahey immediately hung up the phone. Shortly thereafter he dispatched some compliant priests to persuade Zakaria to hand over the recording of the phone conversation. Zakaria advised them it was recorded only in his memory, not on a separate tape. With this restraint removed, the police were free to plot their next move.

A few nights later, at about 11.00p.m., young Peter was the first to be aroused by someone pounding on the front door. Half asleep, all he could grab to repel the would-be intruders was a T-shirt. Quickly he crept to the door and secured the locks, top and bottom. He screamed at whoever was making the racket outside to stop or go away. Obviously neither of those entreaties was about to be accepted. The clamour continued.

Eventually Zakaria and his wife were also awakened. Realising immediately what was about to happen, he raced to his study, retrieved a book he was reading and gave it to his wife to hide. The book was the infamous *Satanic Verses* by Salman Rushdie. Ayatollah Khomeini and his colleagues in Iran, had already issued a fatwa, offering US$5 million to any who succeeded in assassinating the author. When the door was finally opened, about 30 secret police officers and soldiers swarmed into the house and immediately began a thorough search in every room for any incriminating evidence that they could uncover, to support their predetermined outcomes.

Right at that time, another son Ben arrived home. To his surprise the whole house seemed full of angry uniformed men. He noticed one officer was searching through Zakaria's bookshelves in his sister's room. He also glimpsed the offending copy of Satanic Verses half hidden among the clothing. He realised it would only be a matter of time before the book was discovered. But at that same instant, the searching officer was called away by a soldier in an adjacent room. Ben quickly took the book and placed it among those already inspected. Elsewhere, police even searched through the children's pencil cases.

One of these officers noticed two bags next to Zakaria's desk. He asked to examine them. Zakaria placed the first bag on his lap and carefully opened it to reveal the church's marriage registry. Zakaria hoped the officer would overlook the other bag. In it were the files of approximately 300 Muslim converts to Christianity. Each file contained the life history, contact particulars and photographs of each person. To expose that bag and its contents would have led to unmitigated disaster for all concerned. Zakaria prayed.

Within seconds, the officer asked whether or not the second bag had been searched. Unlike a Muslim practice which permits lying under certain conditions, as in this case, to protect the faith and the faithful, Zakaria, although in a position of extreme danger to himself and others, was unable to lie. He acknowledged the bag had not been searched. And he continued to pray.

Slowly he opened the bag and extracted the first book which he handed to the officer. It was a civil marriage Registry book. The exasperated officer asked why Zakaria kept the Registries in different bags. He in turn smilingly replied, that it was a matter of his personal prerogative. He kept the second bag closed and continued to pray. The officer lost interest and went off to search elsewhere.

The object of his search was a taped testimony of a previously very zealous Muslim lady, who was known to have dramatically converted to Christianity. This had caused somewhat of an uproar around Cairo. Obviously the thinking was that Zakaria had been involved somehow.

Looking through Zakaria's bookshelves, the officer eventually came across a series of tapes numbered 1-300. These tapes corresponded with the numbered files in the bag besides Zakaria's desk. This was the audio addition of each convert's testimony. Again Zakaria prayed. The officer ignored the numbered tapes and selected one labelled 'Dr Mohammad Ghason.'

The officer asked Zakaria did he know Dr Ghason. Zakaria replied that he didn't. With a grin and a sense of victory achieved at last, the officer seized upon the tape. He was quite sure that here was the proof for which they had been searching -- namely that Zakaria was guilty of baptising Muslims. Muslims, better than many Christians, realise that one may adopt or express personal beliefs. But, it is baptism of the new believer which represents a complete break with all which has proceeded that act. After that event there can be no turning back. From a Muslim perspective, baptism is the irreversible act of apostasy, a one-way exit from the community's control.

A few days later, Zakaria asked his family if any knew who Dr Ghason was. Older son Feyez laughed as he explained that Dr Ghason was one of his university lecturers. It had been more convenient for him to listen to his lectures on tape rather than attend in person. But the relief of deliverance would be short lived.

Zakaria was soon once more summonsed to the police station for questioning. This time it was to be about one of his better-known books, *God is One in the Trinity*. There were over 5,000 copies of this book in print. Zakaria reminded the investigating officers that they had already searched his house and found no copies of the allegedly offensive material.

From a Muslim perspective, the Christian doctrine of the Trinity is deeply offensive. Hence any book on the subject is also likely to cause offence. The root of the problem is not in what Christians actually believe or teach regarding the Trinity. It is in the misconceived Islamic caricature of the doctrine from which the problem arises.

Muslims are taught that the Christian 'Trinity' consists of God the Father, who had a physical relationship with God the Mother, Mary, who in turn birthed God the Son, Jesus. This false concept is grossly offensive to Christians as well. But where the 'divinely revealed' religion of Islam claims truth for its own version, Christians are left defenceless. Within Islamic theology, the association of another with Allah, which gives the appearance of seeming to have more than one god, is known as 'shirk'. As a protection against the reappearance of idolatry, understandably 'shirk' attracts the harshest penalties under the provisions of Shariah law.

The Quran decrees that at the last judgement, people guilty of this sin, in this case all Christians, will be punished and doomed to hell (Sura 28: 62-67). They are no more than fuel for hell's fires (Sura 21:98). If that is the future state of all Christians, it could be argued that a foretaste on earth, might just be the means of saving them from such a fate and converting them into good Muslims in the process.

The problem with Zakaria's book was not just the contentious subject of the Trinity but to the Muslim mind he had successfully explained the

Trinity by using the Quran. With this new understanding Muslims were now accepting the Christian message which was even more alarming to the authorities.

It was decided that Zakaria be arrested and held for four days till the courts reopened at the conclusion of the Muslim Eid holiday time. Zakaria did not object, but pointedly observed that such action could result in civil unrest for which the officers would bear responsibility. His thousands of followers waiting to hear him preach were unlikely to take kindly to their leader being arrested and held again on unsubstantiated charges.

The police attempted to find another priest who could lead the service at which Zakaria was shortly to preside. None was available. Realising that temporary discretion could be the better part of valour, the police agreed to release Zakaria to conduct his services, on condition that he report back to them in four days.

Zakaria for his part, upon release immediately contacted the Pope, who agreed to meet with him in Alexandria that same day. The Pope reassured Zakaria that he would use his personal authority to resolve the problem. His advice to government would be to remove Zakaria from Egypt. In keeping with the finest European tradition of sending its recalcitrants to faraway places, Australia was chosen as the appropriate destination.

More Convicts for Australia

The Pope issued a letter appointing Zakaria to St George's - not the one in Cairo, but in distant Australia. It was a newly formed church with as yet no priest appointed. An appropriate letter on the church's official letterhead was duly lodged with the Australian Embassy. Eventually, in keeping with regulations relating to such visas, the family was requested to undergo medical examinations. Zakaria became aware that other priests were being granted their visas much more quickly than his. Inquiry revealed that his application was for a three-year work permit, which attracted the same conditions as a visa for immigration. The church in Melbourne agreed to amend their request, reducing it from three years to one.

Zakaria, his wife and young son Peter were granted visas. The older children, all being above 18 years of age, were no longer considered as dependants and therefore did not qualify to travel with their parents. Magdy, a family friend and respected businessman, decided to travel with the family to ensure they were safely settled in Australia. Departure at the airport was emotional, especially for Zakaria's wife, who like any mother, found it difficult to be separated from her children and three grandchildren. As difficult as that may have been, the drama was about to be ramped up another notch.

No sooner had the downsized family entered the plane, stowed their hand luggage safely into the overhead lockers, settled into their seats, fastened their seat belts and readied themselves for take off, when a police officer appeared and requested Zakaria to deplane for reasons of "standard procedures and formalities." Zakaria indicated to his wife and son to come with him. The officer insisted it was only Zakaria they wanted. Zakaria stood his ground and with equal vehemence, insisted his family go with him. They all did.

From Plane to Prison

The police held Zakaria at the airport's security checkpoint until the plane had departed. Their intention had clearly been to separate him from his wife and child. Disappointed and dispirited, the little family returned home while their baggage winged its way to Singapore. To relocate it would take months.

The following Friday was spent rescheduling flights. Zakaria used the delay to baptise a former Muslim businessman who had been referred to him by a mutual friend. Then on the Sunday morning, police arrived at the home to interview Zakaria further. Peter, who was 16 years of age at that time, thinking they looked kinder than other officers he had seen, decided it would be in order to go to church and to meet with his friends. When he returned home, he learned his father had once more been taken away to the police station.

Peter was heartbroken. It took 45 minutes for him to walk to the police station sobbing all the way. He could not forgive himself for leaving his father's side. By the time he arrived it was too late. His father had already been transported back to prison, for a second time.

The investigation was a continuation of that which had been underway for some time, namely the contents and occasion of Zakaria's book, explaining the Christian doctrine of the Trinity, *God is One in the Trinity.* The book was causing horrendous anxiety within the Muslim community. It provided an apologia of the real Christian position using Quranic and other Islamic sources to support the concept. A transcript of the record of interview provides a fascinating insight into the convoluted processes of Muslim thinking, to retain an outcome, otherwise unsustainable through the application of normal logic.

Investigator: "Why did you use verses from the Quran in your book?"

Zakaria: " Some members of the fanatical Muslim groups call us Christian infidels and hence permit our slaughter. I am concerned that such people create religious sedition. In an attempt to protect Egypt from such tragedies I wrote this book to highlight our upright faith!"

Investigator: "Which Quranic verse did you depend on in your book in discussing the Trinity?"

Zakaria: "Surah El Nesaa (Women), which states that Jesus Christ the son of Mary is the prophet of God, his Word and a Spirit from him. This existent God is also Word and Spirit. This is the Trinity."

Investigator: "We have a report from the Islamic university, Al Azhar, confirming that you twisted this verse to imply that it supports the Christian concept of the Trinity. The university's report states that the Quranic phrase 'a word from God' means 'a sign from Allah' and 'a spirit from him' means 'mercy from Allah'."

Zakaria: "I am 55 years old and I have studied Arabic literature, grammar, poetry, analogies and metaphors and I have never heard that 'word' means 'sign' or that 'spirit' means 'mercy'!"

At the police station, an officer had ordered Zakaria into the back of a van. Curiously an open barrel full of tar was positioned beside him. The driver took off like a man demented. He hurled his van recklessly among the traffic. He whizzed around corners so abruptly as to cause the barrel in the back to roll menacingly out of control. Zakaria understood that the intention of the exercise was to cause him serious personal injury or at least to leave him covered in tar. He lay on his back and used his 183 centimetre body to hold the barrel steady against the side with his feet. The officer, realising the barrel was no longer rattling about as before, began to drive even faster.

As ever God was in control. He honours his saints and strengthens them to endure according to need. If, as the Bible records, God could shut the mouths of lions, quench the fury of flames, deliver from the sword and provide for the destitute, persecuted and mistreated (Hebrews 11:34-37), surely he could protect one of his servants from a tar bath or worse. He did. Zakaria arrived this time at the gates of Torah Prison, none the worse for wear.

The charges against him were simple but serious. If they were upheld it could cost him his life. He was accused of causing religious sedition, attacking Islam, degrading the prophet Mohammad and baptising Muslims into the Christian faith. Each of these 'crimes' was sufficient in itself to warrant execution.

When the chief officer of the prison read the charge sheet, he ordered Zakaria's removal immediately. In his opinion, had he not acted, religious zealots already within the prison would have murdered Zakaria before sunrise, had they found out who he was and what the charges were.

The poor van driver went unsuccessfully from prison to prison. None was willing to guarantee Zakaria's safety. Finally El Mahkoom Prison in the suburb of Torah, agreed to receive him.

Upon Zakaria's admission, prison officers ordered him to exchange his black priestly robe for standard prison apparel. Zakaria declined. He pointed out that only convicted criminals were required to wear regulation prison clothes. The officers thereupon decided to withhold food and a mattress from Zakaria until he complied with their wishes. Zakaria was next escorted to a bare cement cell in the 'chastening' block, so named because it was reserved exclusively to accommodate rebellious prisoners.

The procession to the cell was not encouraging. Any person with less courage than Zakaria would have been rightly alarmed. The party was watched by desperate eyes through slits in cell doors. When other prisoners realised the newest addition to their company was a Christian priest, they began loudly chanting Quranic verses slandering Christianity. Throughout the night the cacophony of humiliation continued unabated.

One prisoner at least knew Zakaria personally. He called out, "You are Zakaria Botross. I'll never forget you. I came to see you at St Mark's Church because I wanted to marry a Christian girl and you refused to marry us. I'll teach you a lesson." A warm and friendly welcome indeed!

Prior to admission to El Makhoom, son-in-law Samir had been faithfully following the prison van to see where Zakaria ultimately might be lodged. This was the only way in which others might know where he was. When Zakaria's lodging was finalised, the Pope's secretary was advised and a food parcel was dispatched via a church official. Irrespective of the source, prison officers refused to allow any food to be given to Zakaria. No food, mattress or blankets would be allowed for the duration of his stay.

On the second day, the other prisoners perhaps tiring of their fruitless aggressive threatening chants, fell silent. Zakaria felt the cell he was in could be his last before his life was ended. There was absolutely nothing in the cell apart from a small piece of loosened limestone. This he used to scratch a Bible verse on the wall, as testimony to his life and the stand he had taken. 'You would have no power over me if it were not given to you from above' (John 19:11). These were the final words of Jesus to Governor Pilate, before he also was taken out and killed. While Zakaria waited, he spent his days in worship, adoring God and submitting his will totally to that of his creator.

Around the world, as word spread of Zakaria's precarious predicament, individual believers in churches commenced a ceaseless chorus of intercession on his behalf. Fr Bishoy Yassa in Sydney called his congregation to a three-day fast. Members of the Coptic Church in Australia petitioned the Egyptian ambassador in Canberra. In Egypt, the Pope was in direct contact with President Hosni Mubarak. The courts eventually decreed that should 1,000 pounds be paid on Zakaria's behalf, he could be favoured by being exiled from Egypt.

On the fourth day of imprisonment Zakaria was released. As he walked through the cell block, prisoners who had cursed him on the way in, now verbally assaulted police officers who were escorting him on the way out. They entitled Zakaria, 'Abu El Zomal' which means 'friend of ours'! In the intervening period, they had learned that Zakaria had previously been imprisoned. According to the prison code of ethics, this entitled Zakaria to be respected as one of them.

New prisoners were referred to as 'khaki'. Zakaria had now attained the highly respected rank of 'swabek' - an experienced prisoner.

As Zakaria was driven out of the prison, one of the officers asked who his mediator was, because the authorities had commanded him to treat Zakaria with the utmost respect. Zakaria advised the guard that his mediator was someone who lived in the blue dome above.

Everyone was excited to have Zakaria home again. Family and friends organised for him and his wife to leave Egypt at the earliest opportunity. To prevent a repetition of what had happened before, the secret police were advised that the couple were booked to depart much later than was the case. It worked. This time they departed without further incident. Businessman Magdy and young son Peter followed the next day. The day after that they all met in Bangkok and proceeded to Melbourne, Australia. They arrived on November 5, 1989.

Zakaria's brother-in-law, Phillip, had lived in Sydney since the 1970s. He used to visit his Cairo relatives regularly. Whenever he did, according to custom, he always brought lots of presents. Peter, the sole remaining dependent child, regarded Australia as a sort of present heaven on earth. He longed to go there. Now without any effort on his part he had arrived. At 16 years of age, he and his parents readied themselves to commence a totally different life in this strange and distant land, 'Down Under'.

CHAPTER 11

EXILED IN AUSTRALIA

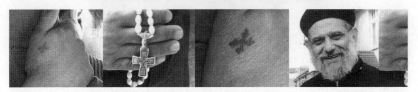

Australia has a long tradition of receiving other nations' unwanted or fleeing citizens. European settlement commenced with the first sailing ships loaded with British convicts which arrived in 1788, to establish what today is known as Sydney. With few exceptions, each of the continent's major coastal capital cities and its major offshore islands originally were populated in this way. Today it continues the tradition. Each year it absorbs among the highest national per capita number of refugees of any nation in the world. One family from Egypt would represent just three more people fleeing persecution or other troubles.

It was late at night on November 5, 1989 when Zakaria, his wife and teenage son Peter, arrived in the southern city of Melbourne after a nine-hour flight from Bangkok. As the heat of the Australian summer built through November, in every sense of the word, they were warmly welcomed.

In bygone years the night of November 5 was an evening to which all Australian children looked forward. Lighting large bonfires, firing off rockets, letting off crackers and all manner of fireworks, the night's celebration was similar to the way in which Chinese people celebrate their New Year. The annual occasion was to commemorate Guy Fawkes' unsuccessful attempt to explode barrels of gunpowder under the British Houses of Parliament on November 1605.

Today, thanks to government safety standards, life is much duller than in Guy Fawkes' time. The Botross family's arrival created no extra fireworks. However, given Zakaria's propensity for boldly standing for the truth as he understood it, he was well able to manufacture his own. It would not be that long in happening.

Suburban Settlers

Upon the family's clearing immigration and customs, they were whisked away to St Mary's Church in the suburb of Kensington, for a time of prayer and thanksgiving. This was led by Bishop Isaiah. They were driven to their new home in Fox Street in the nearby suburb of Saint Albans. Church families had filled the refrigerator and cupboards with food. The family was somewhat overwhelmed by the generosity of these people whom they had never met. Compared with their crowded accommodation in Cairo, this house seemed so spacious and clean with its large living room, kitchen, main bedroom, a smaller bedroom with two beds and another room to be used exclusively for a study. The study was a novel and very welcome experience for Zakaria.

On the first Sunday night in their new country, the slightly bewildered travellers were officially welcomed as chief guests at a celebration held in a rented hall. Bishop Isaiah and other Coptic priests in Melbourne were in attendance and spoke appropriately. Zakaria also gave a speech regarding his hopes for the future direction of his ministry in Melbourne. He said his focus would be on evangelism (Mark 16:15) and discipleship (Matthew 28:20). The Lord had commissioned his Church to follow his example, to preach good news and all that that entailed (Luke 4:18-19) so that humanity could be reconciled with God (2 Corinthians 5:19-20). The Church is also commanded to make disciples, who of themselves would multiply by making other disciples (2 Timothy 2:2).

But the congregation did not have a place of its own in which to worship. They hired school buildings in Leicester Street and Gum Road in St Albans. Later, they rented a hall from the Anglican (Episcopalian) Church in Miller Street, in the suburb of Deer Park.

Zakaria immediately began a weekly Sunday night youth meeting. His son Peter led worship. He had recently made his own personal commitment to follow Jesus. His role was to teach English speaking youth of Middle Eastern origin to sing hymns in Arabic. They learned fast. God moved powerfully among young Coptic Christians who had avoided the Church of their parents' tradition. They started to crowd into the youth meetings.

The meetings had three elements: worship, verse by verse Bible study from the Gospel of John and a message from Zakaria. The youth loved their new pastor. He was so friendly, practical and he spoke to their needs. He visited their homes, learned their names, listened to their stories, helped them with their life issues and had fun with them. Zakaria gave as good as he got. When one of the youth mimicked Zakaria's Egyptian accent, Zakaria bested him with witty comment. Never again was there any problem with lack of respect.

> Zakaria's focus on the necessity for conversion, led many people who had just attended church, into a living personal relationship with Jesus.

Zakaria's focus on the necessity for conversion, led many people who had just attended church, into a living personal relationship with Jesus. He preached a simple gospel and encouraged people to read the Bible for themselves. He was wired and fired to see everyone saved as the Bible made clear they should be. He adopted a schedule which had him visiting every family in the church within three months. The sheer pace which he had set for himself meant he would often arrive home late at night too tired to go to bed. Where he sat down, there he fell asleep.

At the conclusion of each Sunday service, he phoned every congregant who had been absent. He made no notes, but obviously his keenly observant eye, along with his superb memory made it all possible to do.

He worked relentlessly, preaching every Sunday, giving Bible studies every Wednesday and Saturday night, visiting every other night, chairing committee meetings and running camps where appropriate. On Wednesdays he taught from the book of Daniel and on Saturdays from Revelation. The people responded. As word spread within the Coptic community, they started to travel long distances across the city to soak up the Word of God. They'd never experienced anything like this before.

When Zakaria discovered the door-to-door activities of certain sub-Christian-cults, he developed a 10 lesson series to expose their errors and to protect his people from their seductive heresies. Quickly the Church became packed. The love of God, His Word and His ways had been transfused through Zakaria into the people.

Cars and Other Items

Zakaria was sometimes so heavenly minded as to be of little earthly use. Driving a car was one worldly practice which could not be avoided. Back in Cairo a supporter had generously provided Zakaria with his first car. It was a brand new imported Volkswagen sedan. To collect it, Zakaria had to go to Alexandria and drive it back along the highway which connected the two cities. Normally this should have been a journey of about three hours duration. In this case there was a minor challenge to be overcome. Zakaria had never before driven a car in his entire life.

Never one to avoid tackling a problem head-on, Zakaria calmly loaded his brother Francis into the back seat and his sister-in-law Badia into the front seat beside him. Confidently he started the engine and headed out with almost as much skill as many other motorists seem to exhibit on Egyptian highways. With the accelerator almost flattened to the floor, they sped along as if on some famed German autobahn that had no speed limits.

This presented a new problem. How does one avoid slower moving vehicles -- in particular one which has already slowed down to turn off the highway? The obvious answer is to slow one's own vehicle by braking. Precisely the same conclusion was reached by the now slightly experienced but totally untaught Zakaria.

He slammed on the brakes with such force as to lock the wheels and send the car into a spin. The Volkswagen's famous roadholding ability was no match for Zakaria's skill as a would-be pilot. The vehicle took off like a spinning top, flipped upside down and landed on its roof in a nearby canal. Unfortunately, in the absence of water to cushion the landing, rocks had to suffice.

Francis was thrown from the back to the front seat jamming Zakaria hard against the steering wheel. Francis was amazingly uninjured. But Badia sustained whiplash to her neck and Zakaria had broken ribs which kept him bedridden for months. That car, like its driver, also needed time for repair, rest and recuperation.

When Zakaria recovered, by habit he continued to drive fast, perhaps as a reflection of the speed at which his mind always worked. It was often a faith building exercise for his passengers, to realise God had answered their fervent prayer and that once more he had overruled his servant's kamikaze driving tendencies and had brought all safely to their destination.

But in such matters, at least one should not presume upon the Lord's faithfulness forever. God himself had to speak to his modern Jehu, of ancient Biblical fame, about his driving habits. When Zakaria was preparing a study on faithfulness, God brought to his attention the importance of abiding by the speed limits - faithfully!

Driving in Australia was quite a different experience from that in Egypt. To obtain an Australian driving license, the government required a tough driving test to be passed. It consisted of two parts, a written examination regarding rules of the road and a practical test actually out on the road behind the steering wheel of a car. The first part of the test Zakaria passed quite easily. Years of constant study enabled him to learn the new rules and pass the test with flying colours. The practical part should not have been a problem, especially as he had negotiated Egyptian traffic for years without life-threatening incidents.

Unfortunately, Australian practice demanded that all vehicles keep to one side of the road, unless it was safe to overtake. The whole of the road was not available at all times to all drivers to beat all other drivers to whatever space there was between vehicles heading in all directions. To Zakaria's surprise, no sooner had he steered his car onto the road, than the testing officer ordered him to stop. He was failed immediately for driving on the wrong side of the road. A small point had been overlooked by Zakaria. In Egypt should drivers choose to obey the law, they were supposed to drive on the right hand side of the road. In Australia it was on the left.

When Zakaria eventually obtained his license, one new concept he never forgot. It's better to arrive late than dead on time. Therefore if he felt sleepy while driving, he would pull over, take a nap and continue on his way refreshed. When Zakaria was driving a youth leader named Reaf to his home, he suddenly turned off the road, stopped the car in the middle of nowhere, adjusted his seat and fell asleep without saying a single word. Reaf was shocked and alarmed. He didn't know what to do in this seeming emergency. However a few minutes later Zakaria woke up, rubbed his eyes and with renewed energy took off along the highway. Shortly thereafter Reaf gave his life to God. Perhaps Zakaria's driving habits had persuaded him of the advantages of eternal insurance.

St George's youth group quickly grew to about 70 people. Other Coptic churches each retained a mere handful. Jealousy arose. One priest asked Zakaria how he was able to attract so many English speaking youth, when he talked to them only in Arabic. The question was not intended to be complimentary. It had the effect of stirring Zakaria to put his 30 year knowledge of written English into oral practice. From then on he conducted all youth meetings in English.

After the first year in Melbourne, Zakaria and the church secretary of the time, Mr Kozman, lodged an application with the immigration Department for permanent residency in Australia. The department declined the applications. They advised that Zakaria and his family would have to return to Egypt and make application from there. Zakaria explained the potential danger to him personally in returning to Egypt. The departmental officer next advised that Zakaria travel to Singapore to renew the family's current visas there. The risk in pursuing that option was the possibility that the re-entry visas could be denied, thus leaving the family stranded.

When Mr Kozman asked for reasons for these bureaucratic complications, the officer simply asked whether or not all the members of the congregation were in favour of Zakaria remaining as their pastor and priest. Without hesitation Kozman answered in the affirmative.

A few weeks, later when Zakaria was at Melbourne airport's international terminal to farewell a member of his congregation, who was travelling abroad, he coincidentally met the same immigration officer. The man introduced his children to Zakaria, who spontaneously reached into his pocket and gave them some small gifts he was carrying. For the children, this long bearded individual dispensing gifts may have seemed like Santa, except that his flowing robes were not red but black. The adults exchanged pleasantries and moved on.

Shortly afterwards the off duty officer returned and shared information with Zakaria, which strictly speaking, was confidential to the department. The officer advised Zakaria that two people from the church board had visited the immigration office and had submitted a report against Zakaria being granted permanent residency. They were of the opinion that once he gained the permanent residency status, he would no longer submit to the congregation. The cooperative officer suggested a way around this adverse report would be for Zakaria to apply for an extension of his one year visa and following that, resubmit an application for permanent residency. Whatever were the arcane demands of bureaucratic processes which needed to be satisfied, the suggested procedures were followed and were successful.

Journeys of Discovery

On February 5, 1991, Pope Shenouda III donated $10,000 for Zakaria to commence ministry among Australian aboriginals. Zakaria immediately began research into aboriginal history, culture, contemporary lifestyle and related issues. He met with others already working among these people. He travelled to distant places to meet with various aboriginal groups. Two months later, on April 12, he journeyed 600 kilometres northwest of Melbourne to the city of Mildura where he met with local aboriginals. He visited them in their camp and asked why they had not heard about Jesus and Christianity. They explained that they had.

Apparently a Christian missionary had sat with the group years earlier but had suddenly disappeared, never to return. They suspected it may have had something to do with the missionary's introduction of Holy Communion to the group. One of the major social problems faced by aboriginal groups shortly after European settlement in Australia commenced, was that of alcoholism. The missionary introduced the elements of Communion or the Lord's Supper. These are broken bread and a common cup of wine.

Various Christian communities interpret these elements in different ways. They were first introduced by Jesus into what became the earliest Christian community. Basically they are reminders of what happened to Jesus on the cross when he was crucified. His body was broken. His blood was shed.

When the cup of wine was given at the first Communion service conducted by the missionary, the first aboriginal communicant, instead of taking a sip and passing it on to the next person until all had received some, drank the whole lot. This happened on several occasions. It was understandable, given that local aboriginal groups' penchant for quality alcoholic beverages of any sort. To overcome the problem, in an attempt to avoid further increasing the community's problems with alcohol dependency and to try to contextualize the ministry, the missionary replaced wine with tea. This was not favourably received. The missionary ceased to visit the group.

It was not in Zakaria's nature to withdraw when confronted with difficulties. He continued to build relationships, to study aboriginal culture and related issues and to travel extensively to meet with various groups scattered remotely across the vast distances of coastal and inland Australia.

On April 22, 1991, he visited communities in the far north in the city of Townsville, about 3,000 kilometres from his Melbourne base. Approximately 10,000 aboriginals still lived in that city. Zakaria learned that these people were quite reluctant to trust those outside of their kinship groups.

On May 13 of that same year, Zakaria led a ministry team to visit another aboriginal community. This one was in Bairnsdale, approximately 300 kilometres east of Melbourne. During a meeting, Zakaria along with the local pastor, prayed for a demon oppressed man who was delivered. A person who was present had a vision of Jesus helping

Zakaria in this ministry. Demonic activity in Australia is not dissimilar from that in Egypt. Demonic subservience to the person of Jesus is also compellingly the same.

Zakaria continued to meet with aboriginal groups around the State of Victoria and in the city of Melbourne. It became obvious to him that effectiveness in this work would require a person to live among the communities, build relationships, gain respect and trust and then hopefully present the Christian message in a way culturally appropriate to these people groups. But this form of ministry was neither Zakaria's calling nor his gifting. An extensive report of what he had learned and experienced was submitted to the Papal office in Cairo for others to initiate whatever action was deemed appropriate. It was time for Zakaria to try to resolve issues which were affecting the spiritual growth of his Melbourne congregation.

Over and Out

Two of the board members of St George's Church played a dominant role in organising the annual church fete. Throughout the year they recruited others to work hard and contribute toward the big day. But other members of the congregation were less than enthusiastic in responding to the constant pressure upon them.

From a pastoral perspective the 'house of prayer' was looking more like a busy bazaar. People began to complain. Zakaria's heart was for the people to focus primarily on prayer and worship. So probably without due consideration of possible repercussions, he used his authority to cancel the church fete. Organised reaction was swift.

Disaffected board members decided Zakaria should go. They visited parishioners in their homes gathering signatures for a petition to support their case. But insufficient response from church members denied them their hoped-for coup. With the plot now out in the open, Zakaria requested that they reconcile or resign. Three men resigned from the board but not from their goal. They changed tactics.

Using relatives and friends to build a new alliance from which to launch their attack, they levelled unsubstantiated accusations at Zakaria.

They sent letters to the Pope in Egypt requesting Zakaria's removal. Two other Coptic priests were recruited to add weight to their cause. Bishop Moussa who was in Melbourne was approached to attempt to resolve the conflict.

In disputes between pastor and people, central authorities often opt for a compromise of least resistance. Their agenda is usually weighted toward saving the church. Priests and pastors come and go, but the local congregation must remain, in the hope of better outcomes in the future. In Zakaria's case, he took an initiative himself. In July 1991, he wrote to the Pope asking to be transferred to a parish closer to Egypt for the benefit of his immediate family members, whom they had been obliged to leave behind when he had been transferred to Melbourne.

In October 1991 another Bishop happened on the scene. He was visiting Coptic churches mostly in Sydney. Zakaria's supporters urged this Bishop to make a fuller investigation of all which had happened in their attempt to have Zakaria remain with them in Melbourne. He agreed. Having met with all parties to the dispute, he finally called Zakaria, his wife, son and his own secretary, Mr Salama, to a Saturday night meeting. He advised them he had been unable to find a scintilla of evidence to substantiate allegations made against Zakaria. The accusations were false. The family and the secretary were relieved. The secretary was so excited that he phoned others. Some went from house to house to share the good news. By the time Zakaria and his family reached their home, an excited group of well wishers was waiting for them in their driveway. They were delighted that their beloved leader would be staying.

Next morning the Bishop presided over the worship service at Melbourne's main Coptic Church, St Mary's. To the later surprise and shock of Zakaria and to those who had met with him the previous night, the Bishop delivered a verdict contradictory to what he had said the night before. He announced that Zakaria would be transferred.

As soon as Zakaria could, he phoned the Bishop upon his reaching his home, to seek an explanation for the sudden change. None was given. On October 29 1991 the Bishop sent a letter to Zakaria from Sydney commending him for his years of faithful service and in particular his evangelistic fruitfulness. Later it was reported that the Bishop had been offered 'incentives' to change his mind.

Finally in October 1992, Bishop Tadros was sent by the Pope in Egypt to Melbourne, to finalise Zakaria's relocation. He was offered the options of Paris, Canada or Brighton in England. Zakaria's decision was that the last would be first. He opted for Brighton.

Not wanting to cause further emotional distress, particularly to his aggrieved supporters, Zakaria quietly organised his own departure. Apart from his family, no one else was informed of what was about to happen. On October 28, 1992, his son Peter drove him alone to Melbourne airport.

Father and son had left early. In the departure area, they slowly sipped their coffee and talked of intimate issues. Finally, Father and son hugged, cried and parted. Zakaria disappeared behind the frosted automatic doors of the immigration area, to be processed for the long haul from Melbourne to London. Peter wept as he drove slowly back to the now almost empty house which had been their home. For Zakaria it was farewell Australia. Hello England.

CHAPTER 12

SUDAN IN ENGLAND

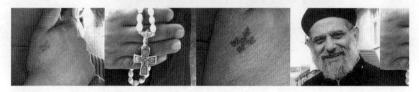

Zakaria's next assignment was to shepherd a small community at Brighton by the sea in southern England. The members were mostly Sudanese refugees. For their Saturday meetings they rented premises from All Saints and St John's Churches. Most lived within a single apartment block which was known as 'Embassy Court'. Zakaria was also located within the same building. For a couple of months he lived alone until his wife could join him. She had remained behind in Melbourne for a couple of months to pack and ship their belongings. She also had to arrange alternate accommodation for their son.

Disappointment

After a year of solid work, Zakaria became disheartened at the comparative lack of spiritual response from among his people. Understandably they were distracted by and focused upon opportunities within their new country of adoption. Materially, for many, compared with life back home or especially with that in refugee camps, they had already arrived in heaven on earth. What could be better than this? These were not the first people, nor would they be the last, to be seduced by materialism or consumed by affluence. The word 'consumerism' took on deeper and more sinister meanings when evaluating their spiritual state. These people were now in the West and like most others within that culture, were besotted by all the ailments of the technocratic, individualised, privatised, but spiritually barren culture of their new environment.

In their anticipation of future material gain, which would surely lead to hitherto undreamed of prosperity, they began neglecting the Word of God. Some had already rejected it. Jesus had warned that it was exceedingly difficult for the rich to enter the kingdom of God (Matthew 19:23-24). Who needs God, when all physical needs are met by personally accumulated wealth or by the safety net of the welfare state?

The observable response to a year of preaching the good news of Jesus, was measured at zero. Zakaria was receiving letters from some members of his congregation who urged briefer sermons. Others suggested their deletion from the church service altogether. These responses would discourage any pulpiteer, not least one who had known extraordinary fruitfulness from this aspect of ministry, in the toughest environments.

One member of the congregation even stood up and interrupted Zakaria, during the delivery of his weekly message. This well-intentioned person demanded Zakaria stop being negative toward the excessive consumption of alcohol and the practice of gambling. Upon Zakaria's requesting him to resume his seat and to save his comments and opinions for more appropriate private conversation after the service, the man exited the church. Thereafter he sent weekly abusive hate mail to Zakaria.

After a year of this seeming barrenness and contention, Zakaria did what many of his profession have done before him. He wrote to his Pope in Egypt requesting a transfer to some other place. From within the dried confines of a field of trampled, crushed dreams, any other pasture looks enticingly green. The Pope did not reply.

While a dispirited Zakaria waited, handcuffed to a declining, disinterested and unresponsive people, he commenced a sermon series on the love of God. One person eventually suggested the sermons ought to be tape recorded. Seizing on that solitary symbol of hope, Zakaria began to fan the flickering flame within this one individual. He met with him regularly and began to disciple him.

Months later the Pope's reply arrived asking Zakaria if he still wished to be relocated. For the sake of the future spiritual well-being of the lone individual who was responding, Zakaria decided to stay on. That person matured to where, in response to God's call upon his life, he was later ordained for ministry. He would not be the only one from that congregation to so respond.

God on the Move

In 1994 Zakaria's son Peter, still back in Australia, felt a prompting of God to join his parents in Brighton for 6 months. He believed he had received a prophecy promising him that wherever he went, there would be fruitfulness and harvest. Upon his arrival, the son shared with the father what he believed the Lord had revealed to him. A dispirited Zakaria received this news with less than characteristic enthusiasm. Two years of hard slog in this barren place did not incline him to optimism. After all, if a very experienced father had failed, what hope could there be for an untried, inexperienced son.

Undaunted, with little more than the zeal of the Lord to commend him, Peter leapt into the work. At the youth meetings he preached a series of messages entitled, *You are Called to be a King.* God used this to light a flame. Ignition was through a single conversion from among the youth. This blazed a trail for others to follow.

Peter quickly organised discipleship groups to conserve the fruit of his evangelism. He introduced prayer vigils. The flickers of new life were fanned into a conflagration. More people were being converted. Peter next moved to include the junior youth department. There he introduced spiritual retreats, interactive Bible studies and concerts of prayer.

The movement intensified. People in holiday hardened Brighton were repenting and returning to God. Almost a hundred small groups were operating. The rented premises of the congregation had to remain open throughout the week to cope with all group gatherings. A place to call their own was needed urgently.

A Home for the Homeless

In Davigdor Road Brighton, Zakaria discovered an empty building awaiting demolition. Formerly it had been known as St Thomas's Church. He agreed to rent it. Within a short while he requested a meeting with the responsible authorities to discuss the possibilities of their selling the property to his growing congregation. A professional survey of the site concluded that the buildings alone would be valued at 500,000 (English) pounds. They would also require immediate attention. An engineering company tendered to carry out the urgently needed structural repairs for 250,000 pounds.

Faith is sometimes spelt R - I - S - K. Zakaria was ever a faith filled pastor to his people. His congregation was 95% refugee asylum seekers. Many were unemployed. Their total resource was meagre indeed. Zakaria was undaunted. Like the boy David who confronted the giant Goliath, he looked not at the size of the problem, but at the bigness of his God.

In a second meeting with the representatives of the owners of the property, Zakaria was asked how much he could actually afford. He avoided a direct answer. He knew that if affordability was based on the church's income, which would be a measure of its ability to repay loans, then the unavoidable conclusion would have to be that his congregations 'affordability' factor would rate as zero. In the preceding 12 months their total income was only 9,000 pounds. They were not yet even in a position to pay Zakaria a full pastoral salary. So, ever the flexible visionary entrepreneur, Zakaria adopted a different approach.

He answered their question with a question of his own. He inquired as to whether or not the church they represented had any involvement in overseas Third World missions. Upon receiving their reply in the affirmative, Zakaria next asked how much they invested in those programs. Members of the group intuitively grasped the implications of his queries. Their reply was to ask was it Zakaria's hope that the property be given as a gift. Zakaria assured them that such was definitely not his intention, but he did want the sellers to view the project within the context of a home-based mission project. He reminded the group that his congregation consisted overwhelmingly of people who had migrated to England as refugees, fleeing religious harassment from an oppressive Islamic regime in their country of origin.

Historically, this sort of harassment or worse, of religious minorities, was well-documented wherever Islam had expanded over the centuries. In such cases, those Christians who declined to convert would at best be reduced to second-class citizens known as dhimmis. They will be forced to pay a tax - Jizya, for the 'privilege' of being 'protected' by Islam. They may be relentlessly pressured and suffer innumerable indignities codified within Islamic law, in a constant attempt to have them 'revert' to Islam. From a Muslim perspective, no one 'converts' to Islam since all are born as Muslims. Some unfortunately slip away from the faith through 'ignorance' until they 'revert'

Faith is sometimes spelt R - I - S - K. Like the boy David who confronted the giant Goliath, Zakariah looked not at the size of the problem, but at the bigness of his God.

In Sudan, open warfare had been waged against non-Muslims by the Islamic government for many years. From this they had fled. It was well publicised common knowledge. Having been accepted into a new country as penniless refugees starting out to rebuild their lives, one of the elements affecting their social cohesion and rehabilitation, was a lack of a place of their own in which to worship. Zakaria asked the sellers if they could not help in some way.

The committee was not averse to such a consideration, but needed assurance that the property, if offered at a reduced price, would in fact be retained as a place of worship and not be opportunistically processed as an investment. Zakaria suggested that a solution could be that a covenant be attached to the deed of sale to the effect that should the property be offered for resale, first right of purchase would belong to the original owners.

Within a week, Zakaria received a letter of offer to sell the land and buildings to his congregation. The stipulated price would not be subject to any further negotiation. It was set at 140,000 pounds. Admittedly the 500,000 pounds worth of buildings needed some 250,000 pounds spent on repairs. But the land alone had been valued at approximately 750,000 pounds. By any calculation, this was an extraordinary offer. It had the perfume of supernatural generosity about it.

Understandably, with excitement and joy, Zakaria replied immediately issuing a letter of acceptance on behalf of the congregation. There remained one small problem. Neither he nor his church had any money with which to finance the deal. To a faith fuelled visionary leader, money is the last and least obstacle to be overcome in any great enterprise for the Kingdom of God.

Within the congregation, there was a Sudanese business entrepreneur who had preceded the more recent wave of refugees who had been washed ashore into Brighton's famous holiday precincts. He had enjoyed the good life in England for many years. He was unique in that within the congregation, he was the only person who had any excess financial capital at his disposal. Surely the Lord had prospered him for such a time as this. Zakaria made an appointment to meet with him.

Zakaria was not intending to ask the businessman for a donation. He only wanted advice on how the church could secure a loan or other line of credit to enable them to proceed with the purchase. Having heard Zakaria's outline of the situation, the man took out his cheque book from his back pocket, wrote and signed a cheque and handed it to Zakaria. Zakaria looked briefly at the cheque. He noted that the 'payee' line was blank and that the cheque was made out for what seemed to be 100 pounds. Zakaria handed the cheque back, assuring the man he personally didn't accept money from anyone. The businessman returned it to Zakaria and insisted he take it and read it properly.

Zakaria countered that he could not understand why the fellow wanted to give a donation of 100 pounds. Again the businessman insisted that Zakaria read the cheque. At last Zakaria realised he just been given a gift of 100,000 pounds! In disbelief he apologised for his mistake.

Next Sunday Zakaria announced to the church the opportunity he'd seized, gave a status report and urged all to support the project according to the financial capacities of each. Obviously it would not be a matter of equal giving, but of equal sacrifice.

Here was an example of a visionary leader, challenging his people to go where they had never been before. It is impossible to cross a chasm with a series of small steps. He challenged them to rise to the occasion. They rose to that challenge. Amazingly the entire purchase price was completely raised within a few months.

Along the way, the process was almost accidentally aborted. Zakaria had accepted the cheque for 100,000 English pounds and placed it in a secure place. Months later, immediately prior to the settlement, neither he nor his wife could remember where it had been placed. An additional anxiety was that no name had been written on the cheque as to whose account it was to be paid. What if someone else had found it, filled in the blank space to benefit themselves, cashed the cheque and absconded with the proceeds? After some days of urgent prayer and patient searching, the cheque was recovered and appropriately used according to the donor's intention.

Next, the structural repairs were completed, not for 250,000 pounds as originally estimated, but for 28,000 pounds. After purchase and structural repairs came refurbishment.

Zakaria, with characteristic zeal, threw himself into the project, fully involving himself in all details and as usual leading by example. He became architect, project manager and unpaid hired labourer. He recruited others to work with him, daily digging, building and painting.

Of great importance in Coptic worship centres, as in most Orthodox traditions, is the use and placement of religious images known as icons. These may be located within an iconostasis or icon bearer. According to church tradition, once in place, this is meant to remain so until the return of Christ. This does not encourage those iconoclasts who might wish to renovate or redecorate the premises in the intervening years.

For making the iconostasis, American oak and French mahogany were selected and shipped to Egypt for the attention of families of specialist woodcarvers, who had inherited their craft through a religious tradition stretching back almost 2,000 years. When their task was complete, the work was shipped in small pieces from Egypt to England, where 40 eager volunteers, reassembled and erected it in just six hours instead of the projected two weeks. At 7.5 metres, it was believed to be the tallest ever built in church history. Within the iconostasis, 24 icons were mounted depicting the last supper, Jesus himself, the Apostles and several Angels. The cost of the iconostasis was 50,000 pounds. The iconic paintings, pews and thick red carpet were also imported from Egypt.

Zakaria was personally involved in another icon - a giant image of Christ painted onto the curved wall behind the altar. It was six metres tall. This was his first attempt at this form of artistic expression.

To prepare, he bought 10 books on teaching one's self to paint, studied them thoroughly and went to work. The end result was stunning. In the process, Zakaria himself almost came to his own end.

Being a man of generous physical proportions, it was not easy for him to work daily for hours twisting to paint on the wall which curved above him. The scaffolding left much to be desired. Several times he fell. Once he fell two metres and struck his head on the marble altar on the way down. That he survived is more testimony to divine protection, than an adherence to appropriate industrial work safety standards.

At last the work was complete and none too soon. The Sudanese congregation of the renamed St Mary and St Abram Coptic Orthodox Church in Davigdor Road, Hove, had grown to 2500 people. Zakaria now had at his disposal, a main auditorium for Sunday and other services, six Sunday school rooms, a secretary's office, a bookshop, a new kitchen and rooms for a visitors' centre and theatre. It was all ready for use for the Orthodox Easter of the year 2,000.

After so much work and extraordinary outcomes, one would expect only blessed times ahead. Not so. From the Garden of Eden onwards, where the blessing of God's presence abounds, Satan will also be attracted for different reasons. St Mary and St Abrams had not escaped his notice. Willing workers to affect his nefarious aims were not that difficult to recruit.

Conflict Again

Back in Sudan, the practice of church government was unbridled democracy. The authority of the congregation was supreme. The priestly role was confined to praying through the liturgy and preaching. According to Egyptian tradition, the priest was in control. This fitted in well with Zakaria's personality and the practice of his leadership. A clash of opposites was not too long in coming.

A minority group who were mostly involved in social activities outside of the church, sought to use church premises for their own financial advantage. They were concluding a sponsorship deal with a British company, in part by saying that the church basement was used as a social club for practising homosexuals.

At last the work was complete and none too soon. The Sudanese congregation had grown to 2500 people.

Upon learning of what was happening, Zakaria intervened immediately to halt proceedings. Stymied from achieving their financial goals, the group next manoeuvred to remove the impediment to their progress - Zakaria himself.

Letters were duly dispatched to influential church leaders requesting Zakaria's relocation. Various allegations were raised including the possibility of Zakaria being a heretic, because he called people to receive Christ personally even though they had been previously 'baptised' as infants.

Eventually they succeeded in recruiting an influential bishop to their cause who in turn, on July 23, 2002 issued a transfer notice for Zakaria to relocate to Denmark. Zakaria declined. He pointed out that he was now nearly 70 years of age and that it was beyond his and his wife's ability to start all over again in a country, culture and language of which he had neither knowledge nor experience. His counter proposal was that should the Pope agree to his being removed from Brighton, he should allow Zakaria to retire from the officially recognised service of priesthood within the church. Priests in the Coptic tradition normally serve for the whole of life. Release from responsibilities through retirement was almost unheard of.

Later that year, during a visit to England, the Pope spoke with Zakaria regarding his retirement proposal. Zakaria assured him that should his request be granted, he would not plant another church. He would confine his activities to developing an internet chat ministry he had been working on through a medium known as PalTalk.

On January 11, 2003 a young Sudanese Bishop arrived in Brighton and requested Zakaria to visit him in the hotel in which he was staying. The bishop advised Zakaria that the Pope had accepted his retirement proposal with immediate effect. He was not even permitted to attend again his beloved church, which he had worked so hard to establish and which had supernaturally flourished under his leadership..

That same night the young bishop visited the church and unleashed unfounded rumours about Zakaria. People who had been converted through Zakaria's ministry, who had known him for 11 years, could not accept the bishop's allegations. His abrupt response was to present his case even more forcefully. The congregation's reaction was to declare a fast and a sit in on the church's premises. From there, events spiralled downward from bad to worse.

Sections of the British media, ever hungry for controversy to create a feeding frenzy of curiosity to sell copy, discovered the story. In the midst of the uproar, the bishop, in an attempt to deflect attention from his own contribution, spread further rumours about Zakaria and others. By this means he had hoped to build support for his position. Instead, it only resulted in a defamation suit being filed against him.

Given the enormous distress this bishop had caused, the Pope back in Egypt wisely decided to replace him with Bishop Paula to try to calm the atmosphere. Three months later the church was still divided and tearing itself apart. A local newspaper, the Argus, reported on April 3 2003, that the police had to be called to quell fighting within the congregation.

Fr Manasa had been sent from Sudan as Zakaria's replacement upon his 'retirement'. Zakaria's supporters were still agitating for his reinstatement. Tempers flared. Blows were struck. The Sussex police intervened but no charges were pressed. A former church secretary reported that the atmosphere in the church had degenerated to the lowest level ever.

Zakaria kept his word and remained distant from the continuing uproar which had resulted directly from his voluntary retirement. In the same month of April, he distanced himself further from the fracas.

To the Land of the Free

For more than three decades Zakaria had been praying about a vision he had for a specialised ministry he wished to develop. An invitation came from people living in United States of America, whom he had personally discipled. This provided the opportunity to organise and commence a new initiative. For two months he remained in the USA and Canada preaching and teaching.

Although during his years in Egypt, he had often been abused and threatened by individual Muslims and had also been unjustly imprisoned and harshly treated by the Islamic dominated government of Egypt, he nevertheless retained a deep and unshakeable love for people of this religion. He believed that the philosophy of their religion and the oppressive societal control which resulted from fundamentals within that religion had entrapped vast numbers of its followers by deception. He longed to see these people at least having an opportunity of choice to respond to Truth as he knew it. This had always been denied them by virtue of the tenets of the religion they were obliged to follow, having been born into Muslim society.

> Zakaria wanted to communicate freely with all Muslims, truth such as it was revealed by Jesus in his teaching and by his person.

Zakaria wanted to communicate freely with all Muslims, truth such as it was revealed by Jesus in his teaching and by his person. He longed to counter the distortion of Christianity which a self-deluded Islam had always preached. He would unravel the historical revisionism, which Islam had long projected to support its unfounded claims.

To confront Islam with its own inconsistencies would not be a 'safe' ministry. Islam does not encourage debate about its claims even by its own followers. It certainly was unlikely to tolerate adverse comment by one outside its ranks. Too many had been threatened or killed for similar attempts in the past.

For Zakaria, with his very detailed knowledge of Arabic, the 'heavenly' language of the Quran and Islam, with his years of study of its documents and doctrines, with decades of experience of being confined within its repressive structures, this was the moment for which he had been prepared. Given his person and his past, he was unlikely to resile from the opportunity of this new challenge.

While he was in the USA and preaching, teaching and sharing his life story, he formed the 'Ecumenical Outreach Ministry', an association dedicated to reaching Muslims with truth and good news about Jesus as Zakaria understood it. In June he returned to the UK. By September 2003 he had changed continents again, for the fourth time, this time to the land of the free - America.

CHAPTER 13

FACING THE GIANT

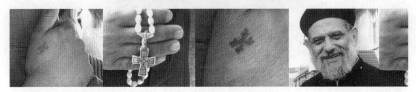

Cyber Battles

Back in 1999 one of Zakaria's friends invited him to participate in Pal Talk. This was an Internet chat room process where Muslims attempted to discredit Christianity with a view to causing Christians to 'revert' to Islam.

One of the common ways in which Muslims attempt to undermine Christian faith, is to cast aspersions as to the veracity of the biblical record in its timeless and current form. Where the Bible and the Quran deal with common historical data and in which there is frequently significant variance between the respective historical accounts, Muslims claim that the reason for the variants, is because Christians and Jews have deliberately changed the original records to hide the truth. Without any evidence to support the Quranic variation, the assertion is made that the Quran is the true record of God's revelation and that the Bible in its present form is merely a hodgepodge of unreliability.

Attempts are made to validate this claim by trying to find inconsistencies within the biblical text. To avoid similar claims against the text of the Quran, of which many could be made, a theory of Abrogation has been developed. Where one passage of the Quran is clearly at variance with another or is contradictory, it is said that the latter revelation from Allah, abrogates or voids the earlier revelation. Critical analysis or comment on the textual veracity of the Quran is variously discouraged or forbidden on pain of death, depending upon the country and the circumstance.

Zakaria, with his lifelong study of the Bible, the Quran and Arabic, enjoyed the challenge of apologetics and debate, given the safety of distance and anonymity which the Internet provided.

On May 23 1999, he launched his own site. It was originally open for just three hours per week from 7.00 to 10.00p.m. G.M.T. each Tuesday. Shortly thereafter, the time was extended to Sunday evenings as well. While many doubted the efficacy of the new medium, Zakaria wasn't one of them. He saw it as an opportunity of great potential, to be used to its maximum. Faith enabled him to see the future as present, the invisible as seen, the impossible as done.

In spite of the hostility toward Zakaria from many of the Muslims who logged onto his site, he was not cowed. He persevered. By 2001 his site was open four days per week. 400 to 500 other people were on line. When debate with Muslim leaders was joined, over 1,000 other participants came on line to listen in.

Zakaria divided his presentations into two distinct sections. Firstly there was the verse by verse exposition of the Bible. This provided explanation, contemplation and application for participants on what Christians believed and how they should behave. Zakaria interestingly commenced by working through Solomon's Song of Songs and the last book in the Bible, Revelation. According to Zakaria, these two books in particular confused many Muslims. He wanted to clarify their meanings and implications.

The second segment of each session was devoted to discussion and issues of comparative religion, during which Zakaria responded to questions from both Christians and Muslims. The earlier debates are still accessible at www.FatherZakaria.com. In all of this, Zakaria's ultimate aim was not to score debating points, but to persuade those with whom he was interfacing, to see that spiritual salvation is found in Jesus Christ alone and it was necessary to respond to that claim accordingly.

Through years of relating to Muslims, Zakaria was able to develop a comprehensive curriculum which answered the most common misconceptions about Christianity which Muslims have been taught by their traditions, religious leaders and sacred texts. The curriculum then went on to raise serious questions about Islam itself.

Zakaria identified 7 issues which Muslims habitually raised by way of objection to Christianity. These were:

1   The Trinity.

The Quran teaches that by 'Trinity' Christians believe that God the Father, who by implication had a physical relationship with God the Mother, that is Mary, produced God the Son and that these three form the Trinity (Surahs 4:169; 5:76-79, 116). This caricature of Biblical truth as Christians understand it is at least as offensive to Christians as to Muslims. Surah 4:171 could be interpreted as carrying a reference to the essential qualities or persons of what Christians call the Trinity:

'Christ Jesus the son of Mary was a Messenger of Allah and his Word, which He bestowed on Mary and a Spirit proceeding from Him'.

2.   The Deity of Christ.

The Quran repeatedly denies this. (Surahs 3:51-52, 72-73; 5:19; 9:90; 19:35-36; 43:57-65). On the other hand, Muslims admit that only God can give life, cause death, provide daily needs and answer prayer, all of which Jesus respectively did. (John 11:38-44; Matthew 21: 18-20; Mark 8: 1-9; John 15: 7, 16; 16:23-24).

3.   The Crucifixion of Christ.

The Quran teaches that Jesus was not crucified. Rather it was another in his likeness. (Surahs 3:47-50; 4:155 - 156). Acceptance of this proposition demolishes the whole purpose of Christ's coming to earth and what was achieved through his life, death and resurrection.

4. The Inspiration of Scripture.

Muslims have a mechanistic understanding of divine inspiration. They believe every word and syllable of the Quran is considered to be precisely existent in the highest heaven. From Allah it was sent down to the lowest heaven and transmitted through an angel Gabriel to Mohammad, "Thus saith the Lord..." is the defining expectation. The Christian Bible, which has so much narrative material, therefore could not be of God. However the Quran declares that it was sent to confirm the preceding Holy Books (Surah 2:89, 91,101) in like manner as the Gospel confirms the Law (Surah 5:46).

5. The Gospel of Barnabas.

This is a spurious document of late origin whose authorship is open to conjecture. In that it supports the Muslim claims of Mohammad's being mentioned in the Bible and Judas being crucified in the place of Jesus, it is thought to be a concoction of a convert to Islam, obviously many centuries removed from the events it purports to record and after the advent of Islam. An Arabic Encyclopaedia confirms that this Gospel was fraudulently composed in the 15th century. (Al Mousoa Al Arabia Al Moyassara, p. 354).

6. Mention of Mohammad in the Bible.

In John's Gospel (14:16, 26; 15:26; 16: 7) where Jesus speaks of the coming of the Comforter or Holy Spirit, that is the Paraclete, which was fulfilled in Acts 2, Muslims claim this to be a reference to Mohammad. This is done by changing the Greek word, 'paraclete' to 'periclyte' which means 'famous, illustrious or praised one'. This allegedly relates to the Arabic meaning behind the name of Mohammad. The writings of Moses (Deuteronomy 18:14-22) are also claimed to refer to the coming of Mohammad. Although the content of that passage makes it impossible to apply to Mohammad, the claim is still made.

7.   Perceived Contradictions in the Bible.

Mostly these arise from an incomplete understanding of the text, context and method of Biblical inspiration.

The second part of Zakaria's curriculum raised questions about Islam itself. These were:

1.   Is the Quran inspired by God?

There is so much at variance with or in direct contradiction to that which God consistently previously revealed in the Jewish and Christian Scriptures. How could God be so inconsistent and still be God? Or are there two different spiritual sources in operation?

2.   Are the Traditions (Hadith) appropriate for a prophet of God?

The tens of thousands of these often contradictory stories, which in some collections have authority almost equal to the Quran itself, are often shocking to the non-initiated reader.

3.   Is Mohammad a prophet at all?

According to Biblical standards the answer would be no. But if one chooses to void the normal meanings associated with the office up to the time of Mohammad, obviously other answers are possible.

If one puts aside Biblical tests to determine authentic prophethood which were devised long before Mohammad's time and instead looks only at his conduct and his life, what do Islamic sources indicate?

According to traditions assembled by Mushnad Ahmad (23302), Mohammad's interests were "women, food and perfume".

He contracted to marry Ayishah when she was 6 years old and consummated the marriage when the girl was 9.

He claimed that Allah instructed him to marry his adopted son's wife, Zeenab. To effect this the son first had to divorce his wife to release her to Mohammad (Surah 33:37).

He taught holy war which historically has been interpreted and overwhelmingly implemented as physical warfare.

> Fight those who believe not in Allah nor the Last Day, nor that forbidden which hath been forbidden by Allah and his Messenger, nor acknowledge the Religion of Truth, from among the People of the Book, until they pay tribute with willing submission and feel themselves subdued (Surah 9:29).

The Traditions record brutalities which normal decorum prevents from mentioning.

To the non-Muslim these and many other episodes cause questions to arise as to how such a one can be described as an authentic Prophet of God.

4. Is the angel Gabriel who is said to have appeared to Mohammad as the medium of revelation for the Quran, actually from God?

> Would it be possible for this 'Being of Light' to bring a revelation in contradiction to all preceding revelations and still be the authentic Gabriel as mentioned in the Bible?

5. Is Allah of the Quran the same as Jehovah of the Bible?

> Comparison of the profiles of the two would seem to indicate that they could be different spiritual entities, regardless of the often repeated Islamic claim that Muslims and Christians worship the same God.

Raising any of these questions which Zakaria addressed in the second part of his curriculum, within an Islamic context, could be dangerous in the extreme. Each year the international media report cases from Muslim countries in particular, where people have had to flee, go into hiding or exile, to save their lives just for being accused of raising queries regarding the fundamentals of Islam. Zakaria's approach in addressing these questions openly and directly was both bold and courageous.

It's not surprising that he was the object of extreme vilification, abuse and aroused hostility, within his own chat room. Fortunately he never responded in kind. He remained calm, thanked his attackers and prayed for them. Many subsequently apologised for their own behaviour.

The Internet ministry continued to grow rapidly through personal recommendation. Christians logged in to Muslim chat rooms and invited them to go to Zakaria's site. Many did and returned repeatedly to participate in inoffensive dialogue, devoid of emotionalism, which calmly explored the dimensions and claims of the world religions of Christianity and Islam.

Zakaria considers that many of the Muslim faith are in a spiritual coma. The claim that their religion is superior to all others is accepted by them, primarily because evaluation or comparative examination is discouraged. When Muslims hear the Christian message, their automatic conclusion is that this is a religion of infidels, a forbidden zone for all Muslims. But often when Muslims are confronted with questions about Islam, the facade of certainty cracks and the search for answers begins.

> Zakaria considers that many of the Muslim faith are in a spiritual coma ... because evaluation or comparative examination is discouraged.

From his extensive interaction with Muslims over many decades, Zakaria estimates that 20 % are fanatical Islamists, 60% are nominal and don't wish to be disturbed to inquire about their own faith and 20 % are sincerely seeking truth beyond the unexamined faith which has been thrust upon them. This last group represents a potential harvest of responsiveness to the Gospel of Jesus, his love, power and grace.

There are many effective ways in which to approach a seeking Muslim. Zakaria's is more along apologetic lines. He seeks to shake assumptions and awaken curiosity. He shakes inquirers' confidence in Islam by highlighting the many contradictions within the Quran and the collections of Traditions. This raises the question that if these obvious inconsistencies are within the sacred records, how could this possibly be sourced from the one true God. If it is not a product of God's revelation, then who really is Allah?

Many Muslim inquirers respond to Zakaria's provoking challenges by crosschecking Islamic sources presented by him, in the hope that he is mistaken. But their search only confirms the accuracy of Zakaria's scholarship and well researched presentations. Often such seekers go one step further and search for answers from their own religious leaders. The result is frequently a hostile, offensive, predictable, counterattack.

A typical example of the process was a Palestinian woman who was studying in the final year at an Islamic religious institution. She inquired of a Sheikh seeking answers to legitimate questions. Every scholar approached gave virtually the same reply, namely that one should avoid thinking about such issues. The student's inquiries from various Sheikhs produced no satisfactory answers. Finally a meeting was scheduled with 15 Sheikhs and the institution's President of the Faculty of Islamic law.

At this meeting the student was asked to present questions. There were only two. Firstly, was it true that Mohammad really participated in a ceremony of marriage to a six-year-old girl? Secondly, did Mohammad sanction Redaat El Kabeer, that is, the act of a woman breast-feeding an adult as a sign of adoption by her?

Although these matters would seem to be well supported by historical evidence, the committee's response was immediate and to a degree, expectedly typical. The President of the Law faculty slapped the enquirer across the face and declared the student to be an infidel. Suspension from the institution was also immediate. That enquirer was later baptised into the Christian faith and is a regular PalTalk participant.

Another enquirer, on becoming aware of these same practices within Islam, also sought confirmation from his own Sheikh. He was advised to desist from his inquiry forthwith. This only served to strengthen his determination to uncover truth for himself. After approaching various religious authorities and sundry institutions, he received advice from one well regarded religious leader, that he should stop listening to comments from or queries raised by Christian 'infidels'.

The enquirer's response was that he didn't care from whom the question arose. He was more interested in finding answers. So resolute was his persistence, that he was eventually deprived of his freedoms by the secret police. His subsequent release was attributed to divine intervention and the realm of the miraculous. Disregarding the extreme danger to his person, he became a Christian and continued to read the proscribed book - the Bible, by torchlight each night huddled under his bed covers. His codename on Pal Talk is 'Farhan' which means 'Joyful'.

When the son of a Sheikh in a European country also heard of the same Islamic practice, he approached his father to confirm or deny the veracity of the reports. His father refused to speak to him for three weeks. Up to that time the father had always given the appearance of being moderate and open-minded. The son was alarmed at the sudden change in his father's behaviour. This Sheikh secluded himself in his office. After three weeks the son observed the father carrying piles of books out of the house and dumping them in the bin. What had happened was that upon receiving his son's question, the Sheikh had done his own research from reliable sources already in his possession. Alarmed and deeply disturbed by the facts he'd uncovered, he concluded that through his own now informed conscience, honesty and integrity demanded he forsake Islam at once. He subsequently confessed faith in Jesus which was acceptable to and adopted by his entire immediate family. They were all baptised.

Later, the former Sheikh's brother was advised of what had transpired. Not uncharacteristically for such cases, the brother, to restore family honour from the shame of apostasy, visited his now Christian brother and stabbed him to death. For this he was sentenced to an extended jail term. The victim's son visited his uncle in prison, extended forgiveness and invited him to consider the claims of Jesus. He who remained physically imprisoned, became spiritually liberated as he accepted Christ in jail. The son remains a regular participant in PalTalk.

PalTalk is an Internet ministry requiring multiple support personnel to facilitate discussion, comment, build relationships and to follow up personally all who make commitments to Jesus and desire to live a life of Christian discipleship. In addition to the principal chat room, other sites are established through which privately, questions are answered, study of the Bible is supported, prayer is offered and preparation for Christian baptism is undertaken. It is a global 'church' without walls.

Zakaria conducts weekly spiritual, educational and technical training sessions for all support staff. In the process, all are acquainted with the apologetics curriculum designed to defend and present Christianity. Also the curriculum instructs in perceived inconsistencies, illogicalities and weak points of Islamic doctrine and practice.

Volunteer helpers follow up all inquirers and converts, strengthening relationships through private discussion, answering all questions and guiding individuals through on-line discipleship courses.

The main web site hosts the complete text of the Bible, sermons, Bible studies, recordings of debates, testimonies of converts from Islam, music, devotional resources for Christians, texts of books written by Zakaria and programs from other satellite channels. By July 2005 the site was receiving 64,000 visits daily. In 2006, 8,000 files were being downloaded daily. Today, web site hits have numbered in excess of 7 million per month.

Seeing is Believing

In 2003 it was decided to video the basic content of PalTalk Internet instruction. Al Hyatt (Life) TV accepted the programs for broadcasting to Europe and the Middle East. Zakaria prepared the first 20 segments which were apologetic, defending the doctrines of the Trinity, the deity of Christ, the inspiration of the Bible and other issues of interest to Muslim viewers. Zakaria's presentations were supported by quotations from the Quran and sundry Islamic scholars. These were broadcast into North Africa and Europe with a special focus on Egypt and Saudi Arabia.

Reactions to the programs varied. Some Muslims protested vigorously. Others welcomed the opportunity to correct distortions about Christianity which had been taught to them by other Muslim scholars. The non-threatening environment of respectful debate provided through the Internet, quickly generated significant response. Zakaria estimates, that in Egypt when he ministered to Muslim inquirers from 1963 to 1989, during that 25 years he saw about 500 Muslims convert to Christianity. Today it is estimated that the rate of conversion is in excess of 1,000 per month. Testimonies from many sources confirm what is happening.

In Bahrain, Christian teaching or fellowship is not readily available for local citizens. A 'Muslim' viewer reported that he and 40 others regularly gather in homes to worship together. All have been converted through watching Zakaria's programs on the Al Hyat channel.

An American medical team dedicated to helping underprivileged people, was surprised when they visited an Egyptian village. The Muslim residents welcomed them by singing Christian songs. They reported that their entire village had become followers of Jesus through watching Zakaria's satellite program.

A young Muslim male in another Egyptian village was partially paralysed. Through watching Zakaria's TV programs he came to understand and appreciate the power of Jesus Christ. One night he prayed, "I realise you are God. Would you be kind enough to heal me?" After falling asleep he had a vivid dream in which Jesus asked him to stretch forth his hand. He did so and was healed immediately. He really was healed. Excitedly when he awoke the next morning he told his parents of his experience and demonstrated the results. Full of joy, they also accepted Jesus as their Lord and Saviour. Other villages reacted, opposing and persecuting the new Christians. They were forced to relocate and were later baptised.

By March 2007 Zakaria had written and recorded 250 episodes of the 28 minute TV programs. Every program is carefully researched by Zakaria himself, using the Quran and commentaries by well-known Islamic scholars. It is a time-consuming process. Those who have lived with Zakaria said he easily copes with the workload getting by with as little as three hours of sleep a night. Programs are filmed against a background of various countries. Zakaria travels to each location and films up to six programs per day.

At the beginning of each day's shoot, the entire film crew of 20 persons gathers for prayer. They ask God to protect all they do, especially the equipment. They pray for error free recording sessions, which might explain why there has hardly ever been a need to double take any episode.

Back in the studio, Zakaria is accompanied by a host or hostess who is normally a convert from Islam. These share their personal testimonies and introduce the discussion topic for the day. It is estimated that in excess of 50 million people watch each episode. Episodes are broadcast four times a day depending on the viewers' convenience of times around the world.

Monthly mail received by the broadcaster in response to the programs was approximately 3,000 letters

Letters and Lives

Not all communications generated through the Internet and TV ministry are complimentary. Some are aggressively hostile. Given Islam's long history of hostility toward and denigration of those of other faiths, such is to be expected. Sometimes this originates from central leadership. At other times it comes from local interaction. However in Zakaria's case, the majority of letters received from ministry are positive, asking for help, seeking answers, raising further questions or recounting their own spiritual journeys.

From right across Islam's heartland response has come. For example -

From a Moroccan:

> I used to hate Christians because I had been taught that they are infidels, polytheists and that they would be the fuel that God would use (for fires) in hell. Your program eliminated all the lies that were injected into my mind and replaced them with the love of Christ. Thank you for showing me the Way.

From an Algerian:

> My grandfather who was the Imam of a mosque, used to take me with him to the mosque every day to recite the Quran. I grew up in a conservative Muslim environment. At age 26 I moved to another country and got married. After one month I managed to convert my wife to Islam. I taught her all the required rituals. My family back in Algeria celebrated this event. 14 months ago I started to watch your program. To my surprise I watched three Algerian men talking nice and comforting words about God. But

when I discovered they were Christians, I got upset and turned the television off. I vowed I would never watch this channel again. But I could not keep my vow. The next time I watched, an elderly man saying things about Islam really shocked me. I turned the TV off again.

A week later I returned to the channel and watched Fr Zakaria Botross. He shocked me by saying, "Regret will not help if it's too late." (His talk) continued to break down my belief in and image of Islam. I ordered a copy of the Bible and started to read it. I found it clear and easy to understand. Last Ramadan (Islam's month of fasting from dawn to dusk each day), I surprised my wife and her family. I was born again (by believing on Jesus). My wife cried and told me that there was nothing in the Quran that touched her heart. It was her love for me that led her to accept Islam. I bought her a copy of the Bible and asked her forgiveness for misleading her and our children in past years.

From a Tunisian:

My 78-year-old father was an Imam (a leader) in a mosque. He raised me as a committed, faithful Muslim. I married a Muslim lady and moved to another country. I was challenged to read the Bible. After I started I was surprised to discover your program on Al-Hyatt TV. These programs led me to enthrone Jesus Christ as my Saviour and Lord. Later my wife followed me.

From an Egyptian:

I have been watching this program and I cannot deny the tremendous impact it has had on me. I desperately needed this program in my life to help me and other Muslims to see the truth clearly. I feel as if I've just been born again and become one of God's children. I approached the church for baptism but they were too afraid. I want to know everything about the Lord who saved me. I want to serve him.

From a Jordanian:

I was born into a Jordanian family. I surrendered my life to the Lord after thirty-two years of being a Muslim. Your program removed the scales from my eyes and enabled me to see Christ as Saviour. One thought completely occupies my mind and that is to serve the one who forgave my sins and filled my life with divine light.

From the United Arab Emirates:

I was born into a committed Muslim family. For the last couple of years I have been watching Al Hyatt TV. In a dream I saw the Lord Jesus inside a crystal house calling me to come in. I was going around this beautiful house trying to find the entrance. Your program motivated me to dig deeper into the foundations of Islam. I ended up completely persuaded that Jesus Christ is the Way, the Truth and the Life. Through your programs I finally entered into the 'crystal house.'

Reaction and Opposition

People who respond in this way, if they could be identified, would be in serious trouble in each of their respective homelands. Islam does not take kindly to any incursions into its tightly held territory. No other comparable internationally legal organisation exists on earth, which threatens its members with death, should they decide to resign their membership. To challenge Islam's hold as boldly as Zakaria has done, requires considerable courage. Reaction is inevitable.

Newspapers across the Arab world, along with many Egyptian TV programs, have vigorously attacked and threatened him. Omar Adeeb's well-known program, *Cairo Today* on an official Egyptian channel, threatened to slice Zakaria to pieces. His outburst can be viewed on www.Father Zakaria.com. Approximately 200 articles in various newspapers, magazines and on the Internet had been published by the end of 2006, attacking Zakaria and his programs. He responded to every article brought to his attention, but only one newspaper published his response. This was *The Immigrant Voice,* published in the USA.

Despite many writers who have attacked Zakaria personally, no one, not even a single Muslim scholar, is known to have attempted to answer the questions raised by him.

In 2006 one scholar did write a series of three books entitled, *The Greatest Debate with Father Zakaria Botross about the Divinity of Christ.* However the author was honest enough to admit that he had not conversed with Zakaria and that the arguments the author had advanced were rather one-sided. Perhaps the author alleged debate with Zakaria because mention of his name sells copy. In one well-known Egyptian newspaper, when Zakaria's name was splashed across its front page, it sold an extra 300,000 copies that day.

> Zakaria's mission to the Islamic world is a reminder of God's great love for these people. God certainly doesn't want to overlook one-fifth of the world's population.

And division

Zakaria's bold approach does not sit comfortably with all Christians. Some, living in Islamic countries, fear that the Muslim community might be provoked to attack them. They have good cause for concern.

Christians in Muslim countries have frequently been adversely affected by religious association, for what happens in non-Muslim countries elsewhere in the world. In 2006 alone, Christians in Muslim countries were attacked, persecuted and even killed for events such as the Danish newspaper cartoons of Islam's prophet, Mohammad; for Pope Benedict's quoting a Middle Age monarch's opinion of Islam; for Western troops being involved in Iraq and Afghanistan.

These Christians believe that the Gospel should be preached, but that no comment should be made about Islam.

In such circumstances, Zakaria would align himself with the apostle Paul. After being persecuted in Philippi, Paul moved on to preach boldly in Thessalonica. When Paul's preaching in Corinth resulted in persecution, he didn't shut down. He persisted.

Jesus of course was Paul's model. It was Jesus who warned of all manner of grave dangers and hardship for his disciples when they took his message to the whole world. Zakaria's mission to the Islamic world is a reminder of God's great love for these people. God certainly doesn't want to overlook one-fifth of the world's population. *'He ...is not wanting anyone to perish'* (2 Peter 3:9).

Conversely, there are other Christians who are delighted with Zakaria's ministry. It has answered their own questions about Islam and provided them with an intellectual framework to stand firm with confidence in their own faith. Because of Christians' growing awareness of and education in Islamic beliefs and practice, the rate of conversion from Christianity to Islam has also been declining significantly. In Egypt this has been dramatically so. These Christians through Zakaria's ministry, have additionally been provided with a tool kit of answers for their sincerely seeking Muslim friends, whose curiosity has been aroused by Zakaria's probing. They have also found new boldness and courage.

CHAPTER 14

TO BE CONTINUED

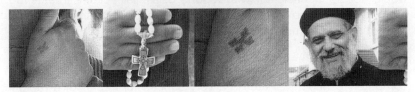

In 1980, Zakaria's son Peter asked him which Apostle he wanted to be like – Peter or Paul. Irrespective of what happened to both of these men at the end of their lives, Zakaria opted for Paul. His reasons were that:

Paul preached the gospel with power.

He discipled his converts.

He wrote letters to instruct emerging churches.

He impacted Christian theology.

He trained leaders to carry on after his departure.

> **If God has done such extraordinary things through an ordinary person like Zakaria, He can certainly do the same through you!**

Today, Zakaria by friend and foe alike might be regarded as a contemporary counterpart of his ancient hero. His ministry is impacting millions. His books have influenced Christian understanding within the Church. His discipleship curricula have become a great resource to train future leaders. One of his passions is to encourage, equip and empower leaders to run as he has run. Through his love, zeal, courage, example and ministry, he increasingly reflects Jesus.

In 1975, Zakaria asked God for a global mission to reach people, especially Muslims, with the gospel of Jesus. After only three decades of testing, the Lord answered Zakaria's prayer. But as in all ministries, it does not come without cost.

Zakaria lives with security at an undisclosed location. The last remaining members of his immediate family have been helped to leave Egypt and live in other countries. Various reports would seem to indicate that there is a multimillion-dollar bounty placed upon Zakaria's life. This would not be inconsistent with reports of similar actions threatened against others who may have incurred the displeasure of various Muslim leaders from time to time.

Zakaria and Violet's children live in three different continents. Janet and Feyez are both involved in helping with PalTalk. Ben assists with computer technology. Peter is a very successful Pastor of a rapidly growing church.

In the Bible there is mention of another person who was also forced to endure Egyptian prison conditions. His name was Joseph. God used that situation to change and prepare Joseph for his future role within the Egyptian government. The chapters of Joseph's life serve as a paradigm of encouragement for many who are called to live and work on tough assignments.

Joseph had a calling on his life from a young age. For reasons he could not understand at the time, he had to endure years of imprisonment. The biblical summary is that God sent Joseph to save his people during great adversity. By way of preparation he was "sold as a slave... bruised...with shackles...put in irons...till the word of the Lord proved him true." (Psalm 105:17-19).

The lesson to be learned from the life of Joseph and the parallels within Zakaria's life is that frequently, between the dream and the diadem there is often the dungeon.

Who knows but for times such as these, if God has not prepared another Joseph, through excruciating experiences, to save people, not from the ravages of drought, but from militant Islam. Irrespective of how long Zakaria lives, undoubtedly his story is to be continued. If God has done such extraordinary things through an ordinary person like Zakaria, He can certainly do the same through you!

To find out more about Father Zakaria's ministry, you are more than welcome to visit his website: http://www.fatherzakaria.com

Ministry resources of books, videos and links can also be resourced in English, Arabic, Italian and French at this website.

CityHarvest
Publications

Books by the same Award Winning Author...

Available online at www.cityharvest.org.au
or order now at all good Christian bookstores.

"No-one has helped us see Islam for what it really is more than Stuart Robinson in his revealing book Mosques and Miracles."

C. PETER WAGNER, CHANCELLOR.
WAGNER LEADERSHIP INSTITUTE. COLORADO
SPRINGS, USA.

"I have read many books on this vital subject, but this was the best."

J. DAVID PAWSON, M.A., B. SC.
BASINGSTOKE, ENGLAND.

"Here at last with encyclopaedic scope, profound Biblical insight and scholarly intellectual balance is the indispensable landmark handbook on Islam..."

MICHAEL CASSIDY, AFRICAN ENTERPRISE.
KWAZULU-NATAL, SOUTH AFRICA.

ISBN: 0957790554

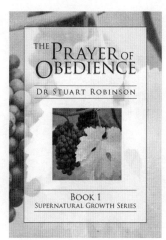

"Just now this is THE book for whole churches to be reading. As a travelling London pastor ... I can personally endorse the integrity of this compelling call to prevailing prayer worldwide."

REV RICHARD BEWES O.B.E.
ALL SOULS CHURCH, LANGHAM PLACE - LONDON

"This book, will motivate you afresh to seek God with your whole heart resulting in a greater dimension of God's power and blessing. I highly recommend it."

MARK CONNER, SENIOR MINISTER,
CITYLIFE CHURCH - MELBOURNE

"To read this book is to be inspired and encouraged to pray persistently, and to watch for God's blessing."

REV DR THE HON. GORDON MOYES, A.C., M.L.C.,
SUPERINTENDENT, WESLEY MISSION - SYDNEY

"The Power Of Vision is a spiritual catalyst, ready and waiting to set off faith explosions in believers. This book offers hope and an unforgettable challenge. In a practical fashion, it also lays out key steps of bringing a God-given vision to glorious birth."

REV DR MARK DURIE, SENIOR MINISTER,
ST MARY'S ANGLICAN CHURCH, CAULFIELD – MELB.

"The Promise Of Vision is a very readable book. It will create a new climate in many churches that results in more people experiencing Kingdom sized visions and dreams."

MURRAY ROBERTSON, SENIOR PASTOR,
SPREYDON BAPTIST CHURCH – CHRISTCHURCH

"Some people see things as they are and ask Why? Stuart Robinson is one of those visionaries who sees things as they could be and asks Why not? He is a visionary dreamer who sees visions and dreams dreams. The Promise Of Vision will inspire and encourage you to become a visionary dreamer as well."

REV ALLAN WEBB, MINISTER AT LARGE,
OMF INTERNATIONAL – SYDNEY

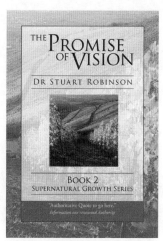